Christian O'Reilly

Is This About Sex?

Me

Published by Methuen Drama 2007

1 3 5 7 9 10 8 6 4 2

Methuen Drama
A & C Black Publishers Limited
38 Soho Square
London W1D 3HB
www.acblack.com

ISBN: 978 1 408 10108 7

A CIP catalogue record for this book
is available from the British Library

Typeset by Country Setting, Kingsdown, Kent

Printed and bound in Great Britain by
CPI Antony Rowe, Chippenham and Eastbourne

Caution

This book is produced using paper that is made from wood grown
in managed, sustainable forests. It is natural, renewable and recyclable.
The logging and manufacturing processes conform to the environmental
regulations of the country of origin.

ROUGH MAGIC IN ASSOCIATION WITH PAVILION THEATRE, DÚN LAOGHAIRE
PRESENTS THE WORLD PREMIÈRE OF

Is this About Sex?

BY CHRISTIAN O'REILLY

Pavilion **Theatre**

IS THIS ABOUT SEX? RECEIVED ITS WORLD PREMIÈRE AT THE TRAVERSE THEATRE, SCOTLAND, ON
2ND AUGUST 2007

ROUGH MAGIC IN ASSOCIATION WITH PAVILION THEATRE, DÚN LAOGHAIRE
PRESENTS THE WORLD PREMIÈRE OF

Is this About Sex?

BY CHRISTIAN O'REILLY

DIRECTOR:	**LYNNE PARKER**
SET DESIGNER:	**PAUL O'MAHONY**
LIGHTING DESIGNER:	**SINÉAD WALLACE**
COSTUME DESIGNER:	**BREEGE FAHY**
PRODUCTION MANAGER:	**PAULA TIERNEY**
STAGE DIRECTOR:	**JUSTIN MURPHY**
STAGE MANAGER:	**ELAINE WALSH**
SET CONSTRUCTION:	**THEATRE PRODUCTION SERVICES**
HAIR & MAKE UP:	**VAL SHERLOCK**
GRAPHIC DESIGN:	**ALPHABET SOUP**
PRODUCTION PHOTOGRAPHY:	**ROS KAVANAGH**
LITERARY MANAGER:	**CHRISTINE MADDEN**
COMPANY MANAGER:	**CLAIRE O'NEILL**
ASSISTANT PRODUCER:	**CIAN O'BRIEN**
PRODUCER:	**DIEGO FASCIATI**

CAST [IN ORDER OF APPEARANCE]

CATHY:	**HILARY O'SHAUGHNESSY**
DANIEL:	**DARRAGH KELLY**
PAUL:	**RORY NOLAN**
ANGELA:	**RUTH HEGARTY**
KAY:	**ALI WHITE**

The performance runs for 1 hour and 45 minutes with no interval.

ROUGH MAGIC WOULD LIKE TO THANK THE FOLLOWING FOR THEIR KIND ASSISTANCE: the Arts Council /An Chomhairle Ealaíon, Culture Ireland, Dún Laoghaire-Rathdown County Council, TEAM Theatre Company, the Abbey Theatre, the Gate Theatre, Smock Alley and all the staff and crew at the Traverse.

Please note that the text of the play, which appears in this volume, may have changed during the rehearsal process and appear in slightly altered form in the performance.

Rough Magic and New Writing

The development and production of new work for the stage lies at the heart of Rough Magic's artistic mission. Founded in 1984, the company began by presenting Irish premières of leading contemporary international plays before beginning to commission and develop new work by Irish playwrights. Since the late 1980s, the company has presented plays by a number of significant writers, such as Pom Boyd, Declan Hughes, Paula Meehan, Gina Moxley, Donal O'Kelly, Morna Regan, Gerald Murphy, Ioanna Anderson and Arthur Riordan; eight of these scripts have been published in the collection **Rough Magic: First Plays** [New Island Books, 1999].

"Few companies set the stage ablaze quite like Rough Magic." *Time Out*

Since the establishment of its Literary Department in 2001, the company continues to commission, develop and present new plays by leading Irish playwrights. Recent productions include **The Bonefire** by Rosemary Jenkinson [Dublin Theatre Festival 2006], **The Sugar Wife** by Elizabeth Kuti [Project Arts Centre 2005, Soho Theatre 2006] and **Improbable Frequency** by Arthur Riordan and Bell Helicopter [Dublin Theatre Festival 2004; Abbey Theatre 2005; Kontakt Festival, Torun, Edinburgh Fringe Festival 2006]. At any one time, the company's programme of new play commissions includes a diverse range of work at various stages of development. Activities undertaken to assist playwrights in their work include critical analysis, support, feedback and discussion through various drafts and workshops with carefully selected casts of exceptional actors.

The Literary Department – comprised of Rough Magic's Literary Manager and a team of capable script assessors who work within the theatre sector – also reads and discusses the many unsolicited scripts submitted to the company. Upon reading and considering the scripts, the Literary Manager provides constructive evaluation, feedback and encouragement to promising Irish playwrights on an ongoing basis. The pool of unsolicited manuscripts in turn can help the company discover new candidates for its ongoing **SEEDS** programme.

In 2001, Rough Magic, in association with the Dublin Fringe Festival, initiated the highly successful **SEEDS** project: a new writing initiative designed to *seek out, encourage, enable, develop* and *stage* new Irish writing. Following the success of the initial project, the company launched a second phase, **SEEDS II**, in 2004. For this second cycle of the **SEEDS** project, the three chosen playwrights were joined by three emerging directors in order to meet the great need for extended professional development in the performing arts. The third phase of the programme, **SEEDS III**, has expanded further to include additional theatre practitioners, such as designers and producers. Each **SEEDS** cycle culminates in a showcase featuring the presentation of a new work by the three currently participating writers in rehearsed readings for the general public. As Rough Magic is committed to the continual development of the performing arts sector to the utmost level of expertise, the company will continue to offer the **SEEDS** initiative, with new writing as an integral component of its programme.

Rough Magic is devoted to furthering and promoting the excellence of Irish playwrighting and will continue to develop not only promising and talented writers but also its support and literary development processes. Feedback and ideas are always welcome. Further information about Rough Magic and its activities is available at **www.rough-magic.com**

"It is a measure of Rough Magic's success over the years, that when it launches a new production, one automatically sits up and takes notice". *Irish Times*

CHRISTIAN O'REILLY WRITER

Christian O'Reilly writes for theatre, film, television and radio. His one-act play, **It Just Came Out**, was staged by Druid as part of its Debut series [2001]. His first full-length play, **The Good Father**, produced by Druid and directed by Garry Hynes [Galway Arts Festival 2002, national tour 2003], was the joint winner of the 2002 Stewart Parker Trust New Playwright Bursary. Other plays include **The Avenue** [St. John's Theatre, Listowel 2005], **Problem Solvers Anonymous** and **It Won't Be Great When I'm Not Here** [Dublin Fringe Festival 2004, national tour 2005]. For youth theatre he has written **Treble**, commissioned by Abbey Outreach, and **Teacher** for Galway Youth Theatre. For radio [RTÉ, Lyric FM, BBC] he has written **The Play, Chapatti, My Spanish Countess Granny** and an adaptation of **The Good Father**. His screen credits include **On Home Ground** [RTÉ], three short films [**The Birthday, The Kiss of Life** and **The Ring**] and **Inside I'm Dancing**, a feature film based on his original story. **Inside I'm Dancing** won the Audience Award for Best Film at the Edinburgh Film Festival [2004] and two Irish Film and Television Awards – Best Script [2004] and the AIB People's Choice Award for Best Irish Film [2005]. Christian lives in Galway with his wife, Ailbhe.

LYNNE PARKER DIRECTOR

Lynne is co-founder and Artistic Director of Rough Magic Theatre Company. Productions for Rough Magic include **Top Girls, Decadence, The Country Wife, Nightshade, Spokesong, Serious Money, Aunt Dan and Lemon, The Tempest, Tom and Viv, Lady Windermere's Fan, Digging for Fire, Love And A Bottle, I Can't Get Started, New Morning, Danti-Dan, Down Onto Blue, The Dogs, Hidden Charges, Halloween Night, The Way Of The World, Pentecost, Northern Star, The School for Scandal, The Whisperers, Boomtown, Three Days of Rain, Dead Funny, Midden** [Fringe First, 2001], **Copenhagen** [Best Production, Irish Times/ESB Irish Theatre Awards], **Shiver, Olga, Take Me Away** [Fringe First, 2004], **Improbable Frequency** [Best Director and Best Production, Irish Times/ESB Irish Theatre Awards], **The Life of Galileo, The Sugar Wife, The Taming of the Shrew, The Bonefire** and **Don Carlos**. Productions at Abbey and Peacock Theatres include **The Trojan Women, The Doctor's Dilemma, Tartuffe, Down the Line, The Sanctuary Lamp, The Drawer Boy** [Galway Arts Festival co-production], **The Shape of Metal** and **Heavenly Bodies** [Best Director, Irish Times/ESB Irish Theatre Awards]. Other work outside the company includes productions for Druid, Tinderbox, Opera Theatre Company and 7:84 Scotland, and Lynne was an associate artist of Charabanc for whom she adapted and directed **The House of Bernarda Alba**. Lynne has also directed **The Clearing** [Bush Theatre]; **The Playboy of the Western World, The Silver Tassie** and **Our Father** [Almeida Theatre]; **Brothers of the Brush** [Arts Theatre]; **The Shadow of a Gunman** [Gate, Dublin]; **Playhouse Creatures** [The Peter Hall Company at the Old Vic]; **The Importance of Being Earnest** [West Yorkshire Playhouse]; **Love Me?!** [The Corn Exchange's Car Show]; **The Comedy of Errors** [RSC]; **Olga** and **Shimmer** [Traverse Theatre]; **The Drunkard** [b*spoke Theatre Company]; **Only The Lonely** [Birmingham Rep] and **Dancing at Lughnasa** [National Theatre of Romania, Bucharest].

RUTH HEGARTY ANGELA

Ruth has previously appeared with Rough Magic in **Attempts on Her Life** and **Midden,** for which she received a Best Actress nomination at the Dublin Fringe Festival Festival 2001. Other theatre credits include **The Buddhist of Castleknock** [Fishamble Theatre Company], **Heartbreak House** [Irish Theatre Company], **Educating Rita** [Gate Theatre], **Play It Again, Sam** [Eblana Theatre], **Tarry Flynn** [Abbey Theatre], **The Communication Cord** [Field Day Theatre Company], **Mother Courage** [Lyceum, Edinburgh]. Film and television credits include **The Life of JM Synge, Caught in a Free Stage, Strumpet City, The Ante Room, Eagles and Trumpets, Da, The War of the Buttons, Glenroe, An Awfully Big Adventure** and **The Last Furlong.**

DARRAGH KELLY DANIEL

Darragh has previously appeared with Rough Magic in **Attempts on Her Life, Don Carlos, The Taming of the Shrew, Improbable Frequency, Words of Advice for Young People, Three Days of Rain, Digging For Fire, Way of The World, Northern Star, School For Scandal, Lady Windermere's Fan** and **Hidden Charges.** Other theatre credits include **All My Sons, The Colleen Bawn, Give me your Answer Do!, The Importance of Being Earnest, Macbeth, Philadelphia, Here I Come!** and **Angels in America** [Abbey]; **Doldrum Bay** [Peacock]; **Hysteria** [b*spoke Theatre Company]; **Our Father** [Almeida]; **Troilus and Cressida** [Oxford Stage]; **Kiss of the Spiderwoman** [Co Motion]; **Brothers of the Brush** [The Arts Centre]; **The Merchant of Venice** [Riverbank]. Film and TV credits include **Paths to Freedom, Veronica Guerin, Intermission, Stew, Ballykissangel, Ailsa, Snakes and Ladders, The General, Nora, Proof, Trouble with Sex** and **Batman Begins.**

RORY NOLAN PAUL

Rory has previously worked with Rough Magic on **Attempts on Her Life, Don Carlos, The Taming of the Shrew, Improbable Frequency** and appeared in **Liliom** as part of the Seeds II Showcase. Other theatre credits include **Woyzeck** [Corcadorca], **Sleeping Beauty** [Landmark Produtions/The Helix], **The Evils of Tobacco** and **The Bear,** for which he was nominated Best Male Performer at the Fringe Festival 2006 [Mangiare], **Dr Ledbetter's Experiment** [The Performance Corporation] **King Ubu** [Fineswine/Galway Arts Festival], **A Christmas Carol** [The Gate], **The Yokohama Delegation** [The Performance Corporation], **Family Stories** [b*spoke], **The Wiremen** [Gaiety], **King Lear** [Second Age], **Heavenly Bodies** [Peacock], **The Drunkard** [b*spoke & Galway Arts Festival], **To Be Confirmed** [Project] and **Nocturne** [Cardboardbox]. Television and radio work includes **Trouble in Paradise** [Great Western] **The King With Horse's Ears** [RTÉ], **Ross O'Carroll Kelly's The Twelve Days of Christmas** [Magpie Productions] and the forthcoming **Baker St. Irregulars** [BBC]. Rory graduated from the Gaiety School of Acting in 2003.

HILARY O'SHAUGHNESSY CATHY

Hilary has previously appeared with Rough Magic in **Attempts on Her Life**. Previous theatre credits include the **Devil's Larder** [Grid Iron Theatre Company] as part of Corcadorca's Relocation Season at the Edinburgh Fringe Festival, where it received a Fringe First, a Herald Angel and Two Total Theatre Awards. She has also worked with Meridian, Asylum, Granary Productions and TEAM. She is co-founder and Joint Artistic Director of Playgroup, and has appeared in **Train Show, Crave** and **Soap!** She was Associate Director on their promenade performance **Dark Week** that received a nomination for the Judges' Special Award at the Irish Times Theatre Awards in 2005. In May 2006, she won a scholarship from the Goethe-Institut to take part in the International Forum of young theatre practitioners as part of the Theatertreffen theatre festival in Berlin. She is currently working on a theatre piece in connection with the Berliner Festspiele and Iranian director Nassirin Pourhosseini and the development of a musical, a new production of **Wuthering Heights** and a guided love tour of Berlin for Playgroup. Hilary is a regular reader for **Book On One** and **Fiction Fifteen** for RTÉ Radio.

ALI WHITE KAY

Ali White has previously worked with Rough Magic on **The School for Scandal, Lady Windermere's Fan** and **Love and a Bottle**. Other theatre credits include at the Abbey Theatre: **Closer**, and **The House** [for which she received an Irish Times Best Supporting Actress Nomination]; **Doldrum Bay; Dancing at Lughnasa, Translations, Philadelphia Here I Come**, and **The Trojan Women**. For the Gate Theatre Dublin: **Catastrophe, Come and Go, Play,** [Beckett Festival at the Barbican]; **A Midsummer Night's Dream, The Double Dealer,** and **Aristocrats**. She has also performed in **The Importance of Being Earnest** [West Yorkshire Playhouse]; **Playhouse Creatures** [The Old Vic]; **The Steward of Christendom** [Out of Joint/The Royal Court]; **The Silver Tassie** [Almeida Theatre]; **Pygmies In The Ruins** [Royal Court]; **Oliver Twist, All Souls' Night, Playboy of the Western World** and **The Importance of Being Earnest** [The Lyric]; **Cheapside** [Druid]; and most recently **How Many Miles to Babylon** [Second Age]. Film and television credits include: **No Tears, When Brendan Met Trudy, A Love Divided, With Or Without You, The Ambassador** and **Flush**. Writing credits include: **Any Time Now** [Comet Films for BBC/RTÉ], **The Clinic** [RTÉ] and **Catching the Fly** [BBC Radio 4].

BREEGE FAHY COSTUME DESIGNER

Breege has designed costumes for numerous productions for An Taibhdhearch in Galway, including **Cré na Cille, An Beal Bocht, Tina Chnámh** and **Gofa**. She has previously worked as a costume supervisor for Rough Magic on **Attempts on Her Life** and **Dream of Autumn**. Work with Druid includes **On Raftery's Hill, The Country Boys, Philadelphia Here I Come** and **As You Like It**. Film and television work includes **The Old Curiosity Shop, P.S. I Love You, The Tudors, Northanger Abbey, Becoming Jane, Whatever Love Means, League of Gentlemen, King Arthur, Bloom, Sinners, Hide and Seek, Proof 2** and **Showbands**.

JUSTIN MURPHY STAGE DIRECTOR

This is Justin's first production with Rough Magic as Stage Director. Previously, as Stage Manager, he has worked on **Dream of Autumn, The Taming of the Shrew, The Sugar Wife, The Life of Galileo, Take Me Away** and **Words of Advice for Young People**. Other productions include **40 Songs of Green** [Barabbas];

Dandelions [Landmark Productions]; **Making History** [Ouroboros]; **Die Drei Pintos, IL Giuramento** and **Sappho** [Wexford Festival Opera]; **La Belle Helene** and **The Marriage of Figaro** [Castleward Opera]; **Our Country's Good** and **The Madras House** [BADA, London]. As a prop buyer, Justin has worked on **Old Times, Betrayal, The Beckett Festival, The Constant Wife** and **Festen** [The Gate]. Most recently, Justin was engaged as Assistant Company Manager for Wexford Festival Opera at Johnstown Castle.

PAUL O'MAHONY SET DESIGNER

Paul has previously worked with Rough Magic on **Don Carlos**. Recent work includes **Blue/Orange, Saved** [Abbey Theatre]; **This is not a Life, Urban Ghosts: Pale Angel** and **Self Accusation**, for which Paul was nominated for the Jayne Snow Award [Bedrock Productions]; **The Country, Blood, Pyrenees** [Hatch Theatre Company & Project]; **Epic, The Green Fool, The Two Houses, Hades** [Upstate Theatre Project]; **Underneath the Lintel** [Landmark Productions]; **Yerma** [NYU]; and **The Strip** [the Samuel Becket Centre]. Paul is a graduate of Dún Laoghaire Institute of Art, Design and Technology where he received a diploma in Fine Art [Sculpture] and a degree in Production Design. He pursued further studies at the Motley Theatre Design Course in London.

PAULA TIERNEY PRODUCTION MANAGER

Paula's previous Rough Magic productions include **Don Carlos, Dream of Autumn, Improbable Frequency, Rough Magic in Rep, Olga, Shiver, Copenhagen, Pentecost, Northern Star, Danti Dan, Hidden Charges, The Dogs** and **Digging for Fire**. A graduate of UCC, Paula has worked on productions for Barabbas, Bickerstaffe, Calypso, CoisCéim, Fishamble, Everyman Palace Cork, Galloglass, the Gate Theatre, Kilkenny Arts Festival, Pan Pan, The Peacock and Second Age. She has toured nationally and internationally with Opera Theatre Company. She was Stage Director at Buxton and Covent Garden Opera Festivals and at home for Opera Ireland and Wexford Festival Opera. Recent productions include **I, Keano** [Lane Productions] and **Rusalka** [Wexford Festival Opera].

SINÉAD WALLACE LIGHTING DESIGNER

Sinéad has previously worked with Rough Magic on **The Bonefire** and **Don Carlos**. Other lighting design credits include **How Did We Get Here?** and **A Thing of Beauty and a Joy Forever** [Ciotóg]; **Urban Ghosts Season: Pale Angel & Self Accusation** and **This Is Not A Life** [Bedrock]; **The Mental** [Little John Nee]; **Pyrenees** [Hatch]; **Saved, A Number, Blue/Orange** and **True West** [Peacock Theatre]; **Woyzeck** [Rough Magic Seeds II]; **Last Call** [TEAM]; and **The Marriage of Figaro** [Royal Irish Academy of Music] [lighting and set design]. Sinéad graduated from Trinity College in 2004 where she studied Drama and Theatre and is a founding member of Randolf SD I The Company for which she has designed lighting for **Eeugh!topia, The Illusion, The Drowned World** and **The Public**.

ELAINE WALSH STAGE MANAGER

This is Elaine's first production with Rough Magic. Previous theatre credits include **Rusalka, Transformations, Penolope** and **La Vestale** [Wexford Opera Festival]; **Blackbird** and **Dandelions** [Landmark Productions]; **The Lion, The Witch and The Wardrobe, The Pide Piper, Aladdin, The Wizard of Oz** and **Frozen** [Cork Opera House]; **The Magic Flute** [Castleward Opera]; **La Bohème, Cornation of Poppea** and **Fidelio** [OTC] and **The Exit Wound** and **The White Lady** [Meridian Theatre Company].

For Rough Magic

ARTISTIC DIRECTOR **LYNNE PARKER**
EXECUTIVE PRODUCER **DIEGO FASCIATI**
COMPANY MANAGER **CLAIRE O'NEILL**
LITERARY MANAGER **CHRISTINE MADDEN**
ASSOCIATE DIRECTOR **TOM CREED**

BOARD OF DIRECTORS:
JOHN O'DONNELL [CHAIR]
PAUL BRADY
JOHN FANNING
DARRAGH KELLY
STEPHEN MCMANUS
PAULINE MCLYNN
GABY SMYTH

ADVISORY COUNCIL:
SIOBHÁN BOURKE
ANNE BYRNE
CATHERINE DONNELLY
DECLAN HUGHES
DARRAGH KELLY
PAULINE MCLYNN
HÉLÈNE MONTAGUE
MARTIN MURPHY
ARTHUR RIORDAN
STANLEY TOWNSEND

ROUGH MAGIC THEATRE COMPANY

5/6 South Great George's Street, Dublin 2, Ireland
T: +353 [0]1 671 9278 **F:** +353 [0]1 671 9301
E: info@rough-magic.com **W:** www.rough-magic.com
Registered number: 122753

Rough Magic gratefully acknowledges the support of the Arts
Council/An Chomhairle Ealaíon, our Patrons, Culture Ireland,
Dublin City Council and Dún Laoghaire-Rathdown County Council.

Is This About Sex?

For Ailbhe

Characters

Cathy
Daniel
Paul
Kay
Angela

Scene One

The lingerie section of a department store. **Cathy** *is tidying the bras on a rack.* **Daniel** *enters. He's wearing a suit. He notices* **Cathy**. *He examines some bras. He gives up. He approaches her. He is nervous, hesitant, polite, very serious.*

Daniel Excuse me.

Cathy Yes?

Daniel I want to try on bras. I want to try on a bra . . . I want to buy a bra. One that fits me. I . . . Do you know what kind would be best?

Cathy *is too taken aback to respond.*

Daniel I haven't worn one before, you see.

Cathy Right . . .

Daniel So I don't know . . . you know.

Cathy Of course. Er . . . I'm sorry – it's for yourself?

Daniel Yes, for me.

Cathy Not for your wife?

Daniel No.

Cathy Or your girlfriend?

Daniel No, my wife.

Cathy Oh, it is for your wife?

Daniel No . . .

Cathy I thought you said –

Daniel No, you said – I thought you were trying to clarify whether I was married or not?

Cathy No . . .

Daniel I mean I have a wife, not a girlfriend.

Cathy It's none of my business.

Daniel   No, but since you ask . . .

Cathy   Okay. Sorry.

Daniel   It's okay.

Cathy   It's none of my business.

Daniel   Yes, but it's alright.

Cathy   Okay, well . . . is it for . . . is it for fancy dress?

Daniel   No . . .

Cathy   No . . . so it's for . . . everyday use?

Daniel   Erm . . . I wouldn't wear it every day.

Cathy   Okay . . .

Daniel   When would I wear it . . . ? I don't really know. I might not wear it much.

Cathy   So maybe something that's not top of the range?

Daniel   Is that how it works – that some are top of the range?

Cathy   It's just if you're not going to wear it much, there's no point spending too much.

Daniel   Well, I want it to be comfortable. I don't believe in short-changing on clothes.

Cathy   Okay, well, how about . . . ?

She looks around at the racks.

Daniel   Obviously I don't have breasts.

Cathy   No . . .

Daniel   As such . . .

Cathy   Okay . . .

Daniel   But some women are quite flat-chested and they wear bras . . . Don't they?

Cathy   That's true . . .

Daniel   Or maybe they don't? Am I being presumptuous?

Cathy   No . . . Well – okay, some very flat-chested women may not, but even they – generally speaking, for modesty reasons –

Daniel   Oh, because of their nipples?

Cathy   Probably that's it.

Daniel   Or if they were wearing a low-cut top . . . I suppose no woman wants to show off her breasts? No, that's stupid – some women do, but . . .

Cathy   Anyway . . .

Daniel   My thinking is, to stuff them with – I dunno – socks?

Cathy   Socks?

Daniel   To see what it's like. Don't worry about the cup size, in other words. I can just put in one more sock or take out a sock. It's more a thing of the size – around my chest. I think that's the main thing to concern yourself with. Well, apart from comfort – I want it to be comfortable, even if I don't wear it much. And the way it looks – I want it to look nice, even if I'm the only one who'll see it.

Cathy   Okay.

Daniel   Maybe a bit lacy.

Cathy   Do you have a colour in mind?

Daniel   A colour . . . ? I think I'd like to try a white one.

Cathy   A white one, alright.

Daniel   Would that be alright?

Cathy   Of course.

Daniel   What kind . . . sorry, if this isn't too personal a question, what kind do you like to wear?

Cathy   I like to wear . . . well, everyone is different.

Daniel   I'm sorry, I shouldn't –

Cathy   No, it's –

Daniel   I could have studied my wife's . . . I could have tried one of hers. I didn't think of it. No, I did think of it. I didn't want to . . . I mean, they're her bras.

Cathy   She wouldn't have lent you one?

Daniel   No. I suppose I want to get my own. I'm sorry for delaying you.

Cathy   It's okay.

Daniel   I don't mind buying a top-of-the-range one. Do you get a commission?

Cathy   A commission? No. I'm paid by the hour.

Daniel   Oh, that's a pity.

Cathy   No, don't worry about it. That's why I'm here – it's my job.

Daniel   You're very kind. Thank you.

Cathy   Why don't I just get you a few to try on?

Daniel   Would you mind?

Cathy   No, that's how it works. Although, you know . . . maybe trying them on – I suppose you need to . . .

Daniel   Is it awkward?

Cathy   It might be.

Daniel   The dressing rooms are for women?

Cathy   They're for women, yes.

Daniel   Okay . . .

Cathy   But if you wanted to bring some home to try – if they don't fit, you could just bring them back in.

Daniel   Would that be the thing to do, do you think?

Cathy   It might be.

Daniel   I don't want to get you into trouble.

Cathy   No, it's alright.

Daniel   You really are very kind.

Cathy   No, I'm . . . I'm just doing my job.

Daniel   It's nice of you not to make me feel strange.

Cathy   Well . . .

Daniel   I don't want to delay you any longer.

Cathy   Why don't I pick three and you can start from there?

Daniel   Okay.

She picks three bras from the racks. She hands them to him.

Cathy   Now, you'll probably need to pay for all three, but if you just want to bring back the two you don't want, you'll get a refund.

Daniel   Thank you.

Cathy (*waiting for him to leave*)   Alright then.

He hesitates, turns, looks helpless.

Daniel   I wondered about . . . I also wondered about some – I don't even know what the right word is . . . panties? Knickers? Underpants doesn't sound right.

Cathy   You want to get some?

Daniel   Silk ones if possible. I hope I'm not pushing my luck?

Cathy   No, it's okay.

Daniel   You're very kind.

Cathy   I hope there isn't a hidden camera?

He is hurt.

Sorry.

He doesn't know what to say. He's embarrassed and hurt.

I didn't mean to hurt your feelings. It's just . . .

Daniel   It's alright.

Cathy   Can we forget I said that? I don't know where it came from.

Daniel   It's understandable.

Cathy   No –

Daniel   You're being too hard on yourself.

Cathy   Why don't I get you some panties?

Daniel   I'd appreciate that.

Cathy   Silk.

Daniel   I don't mind if they're top of the range.

She takes some off the rack. She hands them to him.

Thanks. (*Feeling them.*) These are nice.

Cathy   Yes.

He hesitates, standing there. She's waiting for him to leave.

Well, that should get you started.

Daniel   Yes. It's a start.

Pause.

Cathy   You want a skirt, don't you?

He nods.

The skirts and tops are upstairs.

Daniel   Oh.

He looks vaguely upstairs, but doesn't move.

Cathy   Why don't I just get you three of everything?

Daniel   Would you mind?

Cathy   No. Would you like me to choose them for you?

Daniel   Yes, but . . . well, I want to look sexy.

Cathy   Okay, sexy. What do you mean by sexy?

Daniel   What do I mean?

Cathy   What do you consider sexy? Some women find business suits sexy. Others go for miniskirts, low-cut tops, that kind of thing.

Daniel   Why don't you get me a selection? I'll try them on at home.

Cathy   Okay . . .

Daniel   Shall I come with you?

Cathy   Yes. Why not? We can pretend they're for your wife.

Daniel   Yes . . .

Cathy   If anyone asks, I mean.

Daniel   Yes . . . have you done this before?

Cathy   No.

They exit.

Scene Two

Cathy *is in bed with her boyfriend,* **Paul***. They're both reading. He's engrossed in his book, Diego Maradona's autobiography. She has no interest in hers, a recent Booker winner.*

Cathy   Are you tired?

Paul   Yeah.

Pause. She looks at him. He does not look up from his book.

Cathy   But not that tired?

Paul   Sorry?

Cathy   Well, you're still reading.

Paul   Yeah.

Pause.

Cathy   Which means you can't be that tired.

Paul   No, I'm tired alright.

Pause. He's still reading.

Cathy   Well, of course you're tired, you're bound to be tired – that's why you're in bed.

Paul   Sorry?

Cathy   But you're not too tired to read.

Paul   No, but I'm getting that way.

Cathy   My point is, there are varying degrees of tiredness.

Pause.

Paul   You're obviously awake.

Cathy   Well, I'm awake, but I'm also tired, but not that tired.

Paul   Well, how tired is 'that tired'?

Cathy   I don't know. How tired do *you* think it is?

Paul   Why are we talking about this?

Cathy   I don't know.

Paul   How's your book?

Cathy   Brilliant.

Paul   Good.

He resumes reading.

Cathy   Why do we read when we go to bed?

Paul   It's the only chance we get.

Cathy   But it puts us to sleep.

Paul   Is that a bad thing?

Cathy   Well, do you think it's a bad thing?

Paul   I think it's good to get a good night's sleep. Don't you?

Cathy   Yes, I do.

Paul   And it's nice to read.

Cathy   It can be.

Paul   It broadens the mind and, you know, that stuff.

Cathy   Absolutely.

Paul   So, all in all, I don't see anything wrong with it.

He resumes reading.

Cathy   Do you know what I'd like to do with that book?

He realises she means his book.

I'd like to throw it across the room. In fact, I'd like to throw it out the window. Then I'd like a car to run over it. Then I'd like a bolt of lightning to strike it so that it burst into flames. Then I'd like to throw this book on top of it. Then I'd like to pick up every book in the house and burn them too. Then –

Paul   Alright.

Cathy   I hate reading. I hate books. I want to burn every book in the world.

Paul   Is this about sex?

Cathy   Of course it isn't about sex . . . Why do you think it's about sex?

Paul   Isn't it?

Cathy   No. But why do you . . . okay, you go to bed – we go to bed – we're tired, we've got work in the morning, we want to get a good night's sleep, so we read, knowing it's going to knock us out . . . Why do we . . . why reading? That's my point. Why do we do the one thing we're not fit to do when we go to bed? If we had half as much sex as the amount of books we read . . . don't you see? And it puts us to sleep. A good shag puts me completely to sleep. And you. You're conked out before you've got your jocks back on.

Paul So it is about sex?

Cathy I just think we've got it backwards. I think we should go to bed, have sex and *then* read.

Paul We'd be asleep by then.

Cathy A small sacrifice to make.

Paul But can't we do both?

Cathy But that's the point. We don't.

Paul We do sometimes.

Cathy We read, get tired, fall asleep. What I want to know is why.

Paul I dunno.

Cathy 'I dunno'? Is that the best you can do?

Paul Maybe it's easier to read.

Cathy Easier?

Paul If you're tired, I mean.

Cathy Me?

Paul One.

Cathy Sex isn't difficult.

Paul It's not difficult, no, but . . .

Cathy But what? . . . Paul, but what? When we started going out, it wasn't difficult. When we started going out, any time of the day, you couldn't keep your hands off me.

He sighs.

What's that meant to mean – a sigh?

Paul I'm just thinking how tired we're going to be in the morning.

Cathy   You used to love sex.

Paul   I still do.

Cathy   You'd rather read.

Paul   No, I wouldn't.

Cathy   But if you're choosing to do one thing that puts you to sleep over another thing that puts you to sleep, surely it suggests that you prefer one thing over the other?

Paul   No, it doesn't. All it suggests is a certain habit, a routine.

Cathy   Then let's change that routine. From now on, let's go to bed and make love and to hell with reading.

Paul   Okay.

Cathy   Or we could go to bed earlier?

Paul   Whatever.

Pause. He resumes reading.

Cathy   I just – I start to wonder if you find me attractive any more.

Paul   Of course I find you attractive.

Cathy   Then why don't you want to have sex with me any more? . . . You never initiate it.

Paul   I do sometimes.

Cathy   Not for ages. I'm always the one. I feel like I'm forcing myself on you.

He is silent.

Talk to me, will you?

Paul   When I say it's difficult . . . it's not difficult, but . . . if I'm tired and I'm trying to make you, you know . . .

Cathy   Trying to make me what?

Paul   Trying to . . .

Cathy   Trying to make me come?

Paul   Sometimes it just takes a while, that's all.

Cathy   So what if it takes a while? I'm allowed to have an orgasm, aren't I?

Paul   Of course you are. I want you to. But I just get so tired sometimes. I feel like I'm at it for ages.

Cathy   Well, sometimes it does take a while, but I didn't think you minded. When you're making love, you know, you're giving – both of you – both of us are giving –

Paul   But it's so much easier for you to . . .

Cathy   You just said it was harder.

Paul   For you to make me . . . you know.

Cathy   Have an orgasm? You're allowed to say it, you know. There's nobody watching.

Paul   I mean, it's ridiculous when you think about it. Two minutes for me, twenty for you. How on earth are people meant to achieve simultaneous orgasm –

Cathy   Come at the same time.

Paul   – unless the man holds back until the woman's ready? It's mathematically, physically impossible otherwise.

Cathy   But even if you have to hold back, isn't that part of the pleasure?

Paul   It can be pleasurable, I'm not denying that, it's just when I'm so tired – sometimes I wish I could get you there quicker, that's all.

Cathy   Get it over with, in other words?

Paul   Sometimes I have only so much energy.

Cathy   You'd have more energy if you didn't read.

Paul   You want me for my mind as well as my body.

She glances down at his book.

Cathy   Diego Maradona?

Paul   So?

Cathy   I want you for your heart, too.

Paul   You have my heart.

Pause. He resumes reading.

Cathy   I can get myself there a lot quicker.

He looks at her.

Well, I can.

Paul   Really?

Cathy   I just know my body better, that's all. I know where to touch. I know how fast and how slow. I'm the one that's feeling it, so I know . . . So I'm going to be the best person at it, I suppose.

Paul   How quickly can you . . . ?

Cathy   Sometimes about two minutes, I'd say.

Paul   Two?

Cathy   It varies. I mean, I don't do it much. Sometimes, if you're away, or if you're asleep and I'm wide awake . . .

Paul   You mean I could be in bed beside you?

Cathy   It's a tension release, that's all. You don't mind, do you?

Paul   I'm not sure . . . But two minutes? It takes at least twenty when I'm . . .

Cathy   Not always.

Paul   It does, Cathy, you know it does.

Cathy   It's not like I mind.

Paul   That makes you ten times better at it than I am.

Cathy   Just because it's quicker doesn't make it better.

Paul   What am I doing wrong?

Cathy   You're not doing anything wrong. You're just . . . not me.

Paul   So you're your own best lover?

Cathy   No . . .

Paul   But that's what you're saying. You know your body better than I could ever hope to.

Cathy   But you'll improve. It just takes –

Paul   I'll improve? What is this – some kind of apprenticeship? We're together three years. I thought you thought I was a wonderful lover?

Cathy   You are. You're just not a lover as often as I'd like.

Paul   Yes. Because I'm not as good at it as you are.

Cathy   It's not a competition. And I don't think of myself as a lover to myself. It's just physical. It's just to put myself to sleep sometimes. I'd much rather you did it any day.

Paul   But I'm never going to be as good at it as you are. I mean, I'm not, am I? We might as well admit it.

Cathy   I can't make love on my own. I can only masturbate. It's not the same thing.

Paul   It's still sex, whatever way you look at it.

Cathy   But making love is about . . . it's about the two of us, it's feeling something . . .

Paul   Do you feel love when we make love?

Cathy   Yes. Yes, I do. That's why I like to look at you. Don't you?

Paul   I might feel it afterwards, when I'm spooning you. Or when I'm making dinner for you. But I don't feel it when we're having sex. All I want to do when I'm having sex is come.

Cathy   You want me to come?

Paul   Yes, I want you to come, but mostly I want me to.

Cathy   So you'd be quite happy if I just lay on my back for two minutes while you did your thing?

Paul   To be honest, sometimes I would.

Cathy   That's incredibly selfish.

Paul   Maybe so. But at least it's honest.

Cathy   I can't help the way I'm built. Women are built the way they're built.

Paul   Then why the hell did whoever built them decide to make it so damn difficult to make them come?

Cathy   Maybe because he hoped that whoever had that job would see it as a pleasure and not as a chore.

Paul   Then he shouldn't have built a world that tired them out so much.

Cathy   Don't blame the world. It's nothing to do with the world. The world wasn't so different when we started going out, but you certainly were.

Pause.

Paul   I do love you, you know.

Cathy   Then why won't you show it?

Paul   Why do I have to show it through sex?

Cathy   You don't enjoy it, do you?

Paul   Of course I enjoy it.

Cathy   Only when it's finished . . . What's changed? Why don't you want to do it all the time, like you used to? Surely it was just as 'difficult' then?

Paul   We were discovering each other then. We know each other now.

Cathy   So it's boring? There's nothing else to discover?

Paul   It's just not new any more.

Cathy   Then how can we make it new?

Paul   We can't.

Cathy   We can't? So that's it? For the rest of our lives?

He shrugs.

But can't we at least try freshening it up? What about dressing up?

Paul   It's going to be the same, no matter what we try. We can dress it up whatever way we want, but it's going to be the same.

Cathy   You're bored with me.

Paul   It's not you. It's just . . .

Cathy   The way it is.

Paul   I bet we're not the only ones.

Cathy   That doesn't make me feel any better . . . What if I was to offer you a blowjob?

Paul   I'd probably say yes to a blowjob.

Pause. She sits there, thinking, annoyed. He tries to resume reading.

Why – are you offering?

She shakes her head. He shrugs to himself, returns to his book.

Cathy   How tired are you now?

Paul (*holding up the book*)   Getting there.

Cathy   Do you want to make love?

Paul   Can I just finish this chapter?

Cathy   It's alright. I think I'm tired too.

Paul   Are you sure?

She curls into bed, her back to him.

Cathy   I'm sure.

Scene Three

Cathy *is working in the shop, tidying racks. Two women enter.* **Cathy** *overhears what they're saying, but pretends not to. The women are* **Kay** *and* **Angela**.

Angela   Go on.

Kay   I don't know if I want to.

Angela   She's the one, they said she was the one.

Kay   I don't know if I want to find out.

Angela   You have to find out. You need to know.

Kay   What if I don't want to know?

Angela   Oh, for God's sake, will you just ask her?

Kay   But it's a turning point. This could be a turning point.

Angela   That's not your fault.

Kay   But I don't think I'm ready for a turning point. Can we talk about it over something to eat?

Angela   Excuse me, miss.

Cathy   Yes?

Angela   My friend needs to ask you something. It's a bit delicate.

Kay   I'm sorry to bother you, this is very embarrassing . . .

Angela   Go on. Ask her.

Kay   I was wondering . . . do you sell camping equipment?

Angela   Was there a man in here yesterday buying women's clothes?

Kay   Allegedly.

Angela   Show her the picture.

Kay   Couldn't we just describe him?

Angela   Show her the picture. Show her your wedding portrait.

Angela *tries to take the framed wedding photo out of* **Kay**'s *handbag.* **Kay** *removes it and shows it to* **Cathy**.

Kay   This is the man. This is my husband.

Cathy (*looking at the picture*)   I'm not sure.

Angela   It was only yesterday.

Kay   They get lots of customers. You get lots of customers, don't you?

Angela   Surely they don't get many men buying women's clothes?

Kay   Do you? Maybe they do?

Angela   He was seen leaving the shop with several bags of clothes under his arms.

Cathy   Maybe one of the other girls served him?

Angela   We spoke to two of them and they said that you served him. We showed them the picture.

Cathy   Well, no disrespect to the other girls, but how would they know who I was serving? I don't notice who they're serving.

Angela   One of them said you spent quite a long time with him. The other one said he looked guilty.

Kay   She didn't say 'guilty', she said 'uncomfortable'. But that's only natural. I'm sure men are never relaxed in lingerie departments?

Cathy *hesitates, looks at the picture again.*

Angela   You did serve him, didn't you?

Cathy   My memory isn't the greatest.

Angela   Are you protecting him? Did he bribe you to protect him?

Cathy   No.

Angela   Did you serve him or not?

Cathy   Possibly, I don't know. Why don't you ask *him* about the clothes?

Angela   Why do you think? She's afraid.

Kay   I wish we'd eaten first. I wish we weren't doing this on an empty stomach.

Angela   Don't worry, Kay, we're going to Fintan's as soon as we're finished here and you're having an almond croissant. Heated.

Cathy (*to* **Kay**)   Maybe the clothes are for you?

Kay   My birthday was two months ago. I don't mean he's mean, he's not – he's the most generous man in the world. But he never buys me clothes spontaneously. He wouldn't have a clue what to get me. They're for someone else, aren't they? He asked you to be discreet. He's having an affair.

Cathy   I swear to you, he didn't mention another woman to me.

Angela   Did he buy the clothes or not?

Cathy   I think he might have.

Angela   He might have?

Cathy   He seemed very nice.

Angela   We're not asking you if he's nice.

Kay   But he is very nice.

Angela   How can he be nice? You call this nice?

Kay, *unable to answer, bows her head in sorrow.*

Angela   What did he buy exactly?

Cathy   I don't remember.

Angela   What did he buy?

Cathy   Bras, panties, skirts, tops, blouses, stockings, tights.

Kay   Stockings *and* tights?

Cathy   He wasn't sure which ones . . . He was . . . Yes, he bought both.

Kay   That's a whole wardrobe.

Angela   But what sizes did he buy? What kind of clothes?

Kay   What kind of woman is she?

Cathy   A fairly good-sized one.

Angela   What?

Cathy   Judging by the sizes, I mean.

Kay   He's having an affair with a fat woman?

Cathy   He didn't say anything about that. Maybe you need to talk to him?

Angela   That's exactly what she needs to do.

Kay   I can't believe this is happening.

Cathy   Would you like me to get you a cup of tea, or a chair?

Angela   No, thank you. You've done enough. Come on, Kay, let's leave this place.

Kay   Can we go for something to eat now? I'm feeling a bit weak.

Angela   Of course. You'll need your strength for what lies ahead.

Kay (*to* **Cathy**, *as they leave*)   Thanks for your help.

They leave. Another woman enters. She turns her face away as she passes the two women leaving. She turns and watches them go. She turns to face **Cathy**. *This woman is* **Daniel**, *dressed in women's clothes.*

Daniel   Hello.

Cathy   Hi. Can I help you?

Daniel   That's good. You don't recognise me.

Cathy   Should I?

Daniel   It's probably the wig.

Cathy (*recognition*)   Your wife was just here.

Daniel   I know. Close call. Did she buy anything?

Cathy   She thinks you're having an affair.

Daniel   Why?

Cathy   You were seen leaving here with bags of women's clothes.

Daniel   Oh no.

Cathy   She's going to talk to you, I think.

Daniel   Oh God.

Cathy   At least that other woman wants her to.

Daniel   What do you think I should do?

Cathy   How should I know?

Daniel   Sorry.

Cathy   I didn't tell her the clothes were for you.

Daniel   Oh. Thank you.

Cathy   I'm assuming you don't want her to know?

Daniel   I haven't decided yet. I don't know if I'm ready to tell her.

Cathy   Well, I hope she does talk to you because I didn't enjoy being in the middle.

Daniel   No, I can appreciate that. I'm sorry. I didn't mean to involve you.

Cathy   Well, you didn't involve me.

Daniel   No, I did. When I asked you to help me yesterday – that was involving you. That was making you an accessory.

Cathy   All I did was sell you some clothes. That's not a crime.

Daniel   I just didn't know how else to . . . I didn't know how else to approach it.

Cathy   Why didn't you just use the internet? You could have ordered stuff online.

Daniel   I know. But I wanted . . . I didn't want it to be cold and impersonal. I wanted . . . I didn't want it to be lonely. I know you probably think I'm a . . . I don't know what you think of me, but at least you didn't say it. You could have thrown me out of the shop. You could have called security.

Cathy   You're still a customer.

Daniel   I hope you'll forgive me, but I got something for you.

Cathy   I can't accept a gift.

Daniel   It's only something small. Please.

He hands her the bag. She looks into it. She takes out a box containing a potted plant.

It's an amaryllis. It'll grow quite quickly. It's already potted. It's not too heavy?

Cathy   No.

Daniel   I was going to get you a bottle of wine or a bunch of flowers, but I don't know if you drink or not, or if you do, what you like to drink, and I didn't want to risk getting you a bunch of flowers in case you're in a relationship and it would make your partner suspicious.

Cathy   That's very thoughtful of you. I am in a relationship, but I sometimes buy flowers for myself. I like to have them in the house.

Daniel   So it wouldn't have been strange?

Cathy   No, but this is lovely, thank you.

Daniel   And it won't seem strange to your partner?

Cathy   He won't even notice.

Daniel   Good. You might need to put it into a larger pot when it's fully grown. Sometimes they get top-heavy and topple over.

Cathy   Okay. Thanks.

She puts the box on the floor. He's still there, looking awkward.

I'd better get back to work.

Daniel   I wondered if I might try on another skirt.

Cathy   Try on?

Daniel   I do look like a woman, don't I?

Cathy   Well, er . . .

Daniel   Don't I?

Cathy   I didn't recognise you, that's true, but . . .

Daniel   But I don't look like a woman?

Cathy   Well . . .

Daniel   No, be honest.

Cathy   Well, I thought you were a woman, but I did wonder about your make-up and your dress sense. I'm sorry, I'm being too critical.

Daniel   No, you're not the only one. The security guard looked at me twice. So did a few people on the street. I'm not very convincing, am I?

Cathy   Is that what you want? To look like a woman?

Daniel   I can't explain what I want. But I feel so free wearing these clothes. I feel like a different person.

Cathy   And you want to be a different person?

Daniel   It's just, the person I am . . . He hasn't turned out the way I wanted him to.

Cathy   You're still the same person.

Daniel   Maybe. But when the air blows up my skirt . . . God, what a sensation.

Cathy *laughs. He smiles.*

Daniel   What's your name?

Cathy   Cathy.

Daniel   My name is Daniel.

They shake hands.

Cathy, can I ask you something? Will you teach me how to become a woman?

Cathy   I can't teach you that, no one can teach you that.

Daniel   I'd be happy to pay you.

Cathy   You're missing the point. I can't teach you that.

Daniel   Okay. (*Pause.*) I'll go and look at the skirts. I'm sorry for bothering you – and thank you again.

Cathy   I'm . . . I just wouldn't know where to start.

Daniel   But you already have . . .

Scene Four

A hotel bedroom. **Paul** *is going down on* **Kay**, *who is moaning. His face is under the sheets, so we can't yet see who it is. She reaches down to lift his face to hers.*

Kay   Come here.

Paul   I'm not finished.

Kay   It's alright.

Paul   I want to make you come like this.

He resumes. She checks her watch. She moans another couple of times, then falls silent, practically forgetting about him. He notices the change and looks up.

Why have you stopped?

Kay   What?

Paul   You've stopped – you were making these great sounds.

Kay   Have I? Sorry, that was just an ecstatic silence.

Paul   Was it?

Kay   Oh course. Don't stop, you're amazing.

Paul *grins smugly, reassured.* **Kay** *pushes his head back under the covers. He resumes. She moans to placate him. She looks around and reaches for her handbag, but it's just out of her reach. She looks down at* **Paul** *and continues moaning. She lets out a loud moan at the same time as she shifts position, getting herself closer to her handbag.* **Paul** *is about to look up, but she keeps his head pressed down.*

Kay   Don't stop.

She is able to reach her handbag now. She moans loudly as she unzips it so that he won't hear. She reaches in and retrieves a Crunchie. She is in the process of trying to open it quietly when she suddenly lets out a genuine moan – his tongue has accidentally found her sweet spot – and in her brief ecstasy she drops the Crunchie onto the floor. She reaches desperately for it, but it's well out of her reach. In her disappointment, she forgets to moan.

Paul   You stopped again!

Kay   What? No, that was just more ecstatic silence.

Paul   No, it wasn't. You were faking it.

Kay   I was not.

Paul   That's why you wanted me to stop.

Kay   I didn't – I don't want you to stop. It just doesn't seem fair that you should do all the work.

Paul   But I want to do it. I want to give you an orgasm.

Kay   I know, and that's lovely of you, but there are other ways.

Paul   But what's wrong with the way I'm doing it?

Kay   Nothing. It's just . . .

Paul   What?

Kay   Well, we're . . . it's just that we're on our lunch break.

Paul   So?

Kay   It's just a practical thing. We haven't eaten.

Paul (*indignant*)   What do you think I'm doing?

Kay   We don't have much time, that's all, and I'm –

Paul   I'm getting there, aren't I?

Kay   You're doing your best and it's lovely . . .

Paul   But you're getting closer . . . ? Aren't you . . . ?

Kay   I just need quite a lot of time, that's all. It's my fault. (*Wagging her finger.*) Bad clitoris.

Paul   I'm doing it wrong. I can't believe it. I'm doing it wrong.

He climbs out from between her legs and lies beside her in bed.

Kay   You're not doing it wrong. It's just that . . . Look, this is a terrible thing to ask, but if you insist on continuing with it –

Paul   I do. I'm not going to let this beat me.

Kay   Then would you mind if I ate my lunch while you're . . . (doing it)?

Paul *looks incredulous.*

Kay   It's just that I'm hungry and these sugar lows, they really knock me out. I haven't eaten since breakfast and I only had a slice of apricot and sesame seed toast. I won't get any crumbs on you and I will enjoy it, honestly I will.

Paul   You want to eat your lunch while I'm going down on you?

Kay We both have needs, don't we?

Paul But what about your other needs?

Kay I know, but that's the thing about me. I just have so many needs, all at the same time. I'm an extremely complex and difficult person. You mustn't take it personally.

Paul Oh, go ahead and eat then. Forget about it. Obviously I'm no good at this.

He folds his arms in frustration.

Kay It's not that you're no good at it. I think you're probably too good.

Paul Really?

Kay It's just that – well, I think you're trying a bit too hard. I mean, your tongue must be exhausted?

Paul Don't worry about my tongue. I've got a fit tongue.

Kay Okay, but . . . how can I put this? It's just that at the rate we're going we'd need all afternoon, maybe even all evening. We've got to be back to work in twenty minutes. I'm sorry for being so blunt about it, but there's no point lying to you.

Paul Are you saying you want to end this?

Kay Of course not. I just want to eat my lunch . . . I'm sorry.

Paul This is unbelievable.

Kay Did you bring a sandwich?

Paul No.

Kay Well, can you get one on your way back to work?

Paul I . . .

Kay Do you want half of mine, in other words?

Paul What's in it?

Kay I got it in that new place around the corner from us. Fintan's. They do the most fantastic lunches. This is ciabatta bread with goat's cheese, sun-dried tomato, chorizo, chopped olives, avocado –

Paul   Forget it.

Kay   Look, just have half of it.

Paul   I don't want your bloody sandwich.

Pause.

Kay   I'm sorry.

Paul   We're having an affair, for God's sake.

Kay   Do you want to end it?

Paul   End it? How can we end it? We've only just started it.

Kay   I don't think we have to follow any rules.

Paul   It's not about rules. It's not about sandwiches. It's about . . . it's about not being able to get enough of each other.

Kay   I'm sorry.

Paul   Do you see what I mean?

Kay   Yes, I do. You're right, I'm sorry. I'm obviously not very good at this.

Paul   No, you're fine, you're absolutely fine.

Kay   I've never done this before, you see.

Paul   Neither have I.

Kay   It's inexperience, isn't it?

Paul   I suppose.

Kay   It didn't occur to me that it was inappropriate to eat a sandwich while you were going down on me. Of course it is. I'm sorry.

Paul   It's alright. We're getting to know each other. And I'll be a lot quicker at . . . if, you know . . . with time, I mean.

Kay   It takes practice.

Paul   I'm sure each woman is different.

Kay   My husband took a while at first. He's amazing at it now. But we're together for six years, so he's had a lot of practice.

This troubles **Paul**. *Pause.*

Paul   How amazing is he?

Kay   Well . . . he can get me there in – I mean, it's extraordinary . . . Obviously, he knows my body intimately.

Paul   Of course. Which is how I want to get to know it.

Kay   Yes, yes.

Paul   Don't you?

Kay   Of course. Yes. Do you mind if I eat my sandwich?

Paul   No, eat away.

Kay   Are you sure you won't have some?

Paul   No, I'll get something on the way back.

She starts eating.

So how quickly can he get you there?

Kay   My husband?

Paul   I'm just curious.

Kay   Well, generally it takes a while.

Paul (*pleased*)   Right.

Kay   But that's because he likes to play with me.

Paul   Of course.

Kay   Little flicks of his tongue here and there, my thighs particularly. He likes licking my thighs.

Paul   You have very lickable thighs.

Kay   Thanks.

Paul   I mean, they're not pimply or anything.

Kay   That's a relief.

Paul   Sorry. Go on.

Kay   Where was I?

Paul   You were saying he generally takes a while because he licks your thighs and so on.

Kay   I mean, you don't want to rush it either.

Paul   Of course not.

Kay   But that's the problem with what we have – there just isn't time to savour it.

Paul   That's the thing. I mean, I don't think I was doing anything wrong –

Kay   God, no –

Paul   You know, I was playing with you. I didn't want to rush you into an orgasm. I don't want you to think I'm just some guy who's only after one thing . . . I want this affair to last.

Kay   Well, to be honest – and don't take this the wrong way, because we are still getting to know each other, but you're just not as practised as he is. You couldn't be. He just seems to know my body better than I do. He's creative. Say I was just so horny that I wanted to come straight away – that's what I'd do if I was on my own, say. Well, he'd withdraw his tongue for a few seconds and make me want it even more. Or he'd stop completely and start kissing other parts of my body.

Paul   Your tits? Breasts.

Kay   Not necessarily. That's just so obvious, you see. It's the first place men go for and really there's a lot more to a woman.

Paul   Of course.

Kay   Maybe he'd turn me over and kiss my lower back, or my shoulder, or the backs of my knees, or my ear lobes.

Paul   And you'd like all that?

Kay   Well, of course. I'd love it . . . But you see, that's not practical for us in the time available.

Paul   No . . .

Kay   And in the circumstances we're doing as well as we possibly can.

Paul   Yes.

Kay   And you know what they say about comparisons . . .

Paul   Yes . . . But, okay – say he wasn't playing with you. Say there wasn't much time. What's his fastest ever time?

Kay   Going down on me?

Paul   Yes. From beginning to climax.

Kay   With foreplay before that?

Paul   A bit.

Kay   It's hard to say. It really depends on how aroused I am.

Paul   Has he ever just gone down on you without any foreplay?

Kay   Yes, he has actually. That was amazing. That was a rush.

Paul   Well, how long did that take?

Kay   You know, that was very fast. Three minutes, I'd say. Maybe even two. I mean, I don't know, I wasn't sitting there with a stopwatch.

Paul   Or a sandwich.

Kay   But you mustn't feel bad about it. You mustn't compare yourself.

Paul   Two or three minutes, though. That's impressive.

Kay   He just has more experience with me.

Paul   But how did he get to be so good at it?

Kay   I don't know. You should ask him.

Paul   I'm sure he'd appreciate that.

Kay   He'll be in next week to service the computers. We could have a threesome.

Paul   No thanks. Not my kind of threesome.

Kay   He wouldn't mind. He'd probably give you a blowjob if I asked him to. God, what a horrible thing to say.

Paul   I don't know whether to ask this or not because I don't want you to ask yourself this question, but why . . . if your husband is such a great lover, why are you having an affair?

Kay   I don't know exactly. Maybe because as wonderful as he is, I just don't find him attractive any more.

Paul   Why not?

Kay   Because he's all he is. He's all he ever will be.

Paul   And do you find me attractive?

Kay   Well, I do. Certainly at the moment.

Paul   Just because I'm different? Just because you don't know me?

Kay   Maybe.

Paul   So there could easily come a point when you don't find me attractive any more?

Kay   Is that so surprising? Is that not the fate of any relationship?

Paul   That's kind of a depressing thought.

Kay   I needed a change, that's all. I just find him so . . . This is going to sound strange. I just find him so generous. It's exhausting. He does everything for me – he cooks, he cleans, he does the food shopping, he irons. He gives everything in bed. I mean, he's always going down on me and I can't remember the last time I gave him so much as a handjob. He just makes me feel so guilty. I just thought, if I'm feeling guilty anyway I might as well have an affair.

Paul   Is that why you didn't want me going down on you –
the generosity thing?

Kay   Maybe.

Paul   So if I'd just fucked you, maybe you wouldn't have
given a second thought to your sandwich?

Kay   Well, I might have been thinking about it, but that's just
me. What about you? What's in this for you?

Paul   I just kept seeing you in those short, tight skirts at work,
those silk blouses you like to wear, the high heels, the stockings.

Kay   Tights.

Paul (*disappointed*)   Really?

Kay   Usually. Stockings aren't all that comfortable. I put them
on today for you.

Paul   I couldn't get up from my desk I had such a hard-on.

Kay   So you just wanted to fuck me?

Paul   Yeah.

Kay   And how did the reality measure up to the fantasy?

Paul   Well, in the fantasy you're sitting at your desk, my head
is between your legs and you're having an orgasm.

Kay   So you didn't just want to fuck me? You wanted to give
me an orgasm. Why do men always feel they have to give me
something?

Paul   Don't worry, I'm not that generous.

Kay   Do you feel guilty at all?

Paul   I wasn't planning on getting around to that yet.

Kay   My husband's having an affair as well.

Paul   Really?

Kay   To tell you the truth, I don't blame him. He must have
noticed how distant I've been lately. He's been trying so hard,

being really attentive and caring – whenever he tries to make love to me, I put him off. It's reached the stage where he must think something's wrong with him. But it's only now that I know that he's having an affair that I actually feel guilty. I feel guilty because I drove him to it.

Paul   Well, maybe he drove you to it.

Kay   How? By being himself?

Paul   By being too caring. He may be a great lover, but maybe he's too much of a perfectionist – too predictable.

Kay   Maybe.

Paul   Whereas I, clearly, am completely imperfect.

Kay   Maybe that is refreshing. The truth is, I don't know.

Paul   So you know about his affair, but he doesn't know about yours?

Kay   Another reason to feel guilty.

Paul   What are you going to do?

Kay   My friend wants me to have it out with him.

Paul   She doesn't know about your affair?

Kay   God, no, I wouldn't tell her anything. I'm mad about her, but she's very judgemental. The thing is, if I'm having an affair, I think he's quite entitled to have one, too. Who am I to judge his when he isn't in a position to judge mine, especially when I feel responsible for his?

Paul   I suppose there is a weird logic in that.

Kay   Well, how would you feel if your girlfriend was having an affair?

Paul   I think I'd feel quite angry.

Kay   Well, that makes you a hypocrite.

Paul   She'd be angry if she knew about mine.

Kay   That would make both of you hypocrites.

Paul   I'd be angry because I think I give her all she needs.

Kay   That's quite a claim.

Paul   Well . . . and she still wants more.

Kay   And she doesn't give you all you need?

Paul   Apparently not.

Kay   Do I fill the gap?

Paul   I'm not sure yet.

She kisses him. He becomes aroused. She stops him.

Kay   We'd better get back to work.

Paul   Any chance of a quickie?

She gets out of bed and starts to dress.

Kay   There's always tomorrow.

She discreetly puts the Crunchie back in her bag.

Scene Five

Daniel *and* **Kay** *are in bed together, both reading. He looks at her guiltily. She becomes aware of this and looks at him.*

Daniel   Sorry.

Kay   Did you –

Daniel   No. Nothing.

He resumes reading, but can't ignore the guilt in the room.

How's the book?

Kay   Hmm?

Daniel   Are you enjoying it?

Kay   Very much.

Pause.

Daniel   You were quiet at dinner.

Kay   Was I?

Daniel   Not that it matters.

Kay   I was too busy eating the lovely meal you cooked for me.

Pause.

Daniel   You said work was busy?

Kay   Yeah.

Daniel   Me too.

Kay   Are you finished your book?

Daniel   No. It's good, though. I should really make more time to read.

Kay   Is now not a good time?

Daniel   Oh. Sorry. I'll shut up.

Kay   I'm just in the middle of it and –

Daniel   I know. It's the only chance we get.

Kay   Yeah.

She resumes reading. He starts kissing her on the arm, working his way up to her shoulder. She turns to look at him.

Daniel   Sorry.

She turns back to her book. He resumes reading his.

Kay   It's not that it isn't lovely.

Daniel   No, you're trying to read.

Kay   It's just –

Daniel   No, I know. It's distracting.

Kay   In a nice way, but –

Daniel   Distracting all the same.

Kay   Sorry.

She resumes reading.

Daniel   But in a nice way?

She turns back to him.

I could continue, perhaps? I don't mean interrupt your reading. I mean I could complement it. While your book is stimulating your mind, I could attend to other parts of you that might appreciate stimulation. Parts of you that might feel tense after a long and hard day at work. Parts of you that, once stimulated, might release the necessary hormones to let you relax.

Kay   Why are you so good to me?

Daniel   Because I love you.

Kay   Why do you love me?

Daniel   Because I do. (*Pause.*) Would madam now allow me to complement her reading?

Kay   Madam appreciates the offer, but she's just not in the mood.

Daniel   Would madam allow herself to be transported into the mood?

Kay   I'd just like to read tonight if that's alright.

Daniel   Of course.

Kay   I love you, too, you know.

Daniel   I know.

She turns away to resume reading. He turns away to go to sleep. She looks at him guiltily.

Scene Six

Cathy'*s bedroom.* **Daniel**, *dressed in a silk kimono, sits in front of a mirror as* **Cathy** *applies his make-up. In the course of the scene she dresses him in women's clothes..*

Daniel   I wish I had long hair.

Cathy   You could grow it.

Daniel   It's falling out. It'll have to be wigs, I'm afraid.

Cathy   Do you ever brush your wife's hair?

Daniel   Not for a while, now that you mention it. I was probably doing it wrong.

Cathy   Do you love her, Daniel?

Daniel   Yeah.

Overcome by sadness, he moves away and sits on the bed.

I've betrayed her, you know. I didn't intend to, I wasn't even conscious of it – of who I really was, of what I really am. When we started going out together, I felt such hope. But look at me. My wife married a woman and she didn't even know it.

Cathy   But neither did you.

Daniel   I don't know if I chose this or not. Have I been in denial my entire life?

Cathy   Did you enjoy dressing up when you were a boy?

Daniel   I never thought about it until recently.

Cathy   So it's all quite latent?

Daniel   I must have been in profound denial. My father's very macho, maybe that's what inhibited me. I tried so hard to satisfy Kay, but she obviously knew that it was a lie – she sensed it. Women are so intuitive, aren't they? So the harder I tried to pretend to be something I wasn't, the more she sensed who I really was. If she saw me now, I don't think she'd be in the least surprised. I think it would all suddenly make sense to her. But it would also break her heart. We married three years ago. We should have at least one child by now. It could be too late for her to start a family with anyone else.

Cathy *starts brushing* **Daniel***'s hair.* **Daniel** *is very touched.*

Daniel   There's no point. I don't have enough.

Cathy   Shhh.

Daniel   It feels lovely. Thank you . . . Cathy?

Cathy   Shhh.

Daniel   You've been such a lovely friend to me. I'd be so grateful if you could remain a friend to me.

Cathy   Of course.

Daniel   Even if you think I'm sick or weird or –

Cathy   Stop it, Daniel.

He starts to cry. She cradles his head in her arms.

It's okay. It's okay.

She turns his face to hers, wipes his tears.

I don't think you're sick, I don't think you're weird. You're one of the loveliest people I've ever met.

Daniel   I'm a home-wrecker.

Cathy   You can't help who you are. Your wife may not thank you for it, at least not right away, but she'll know it's for the best.

Daniel   I can't lie to her forever.

Cathy   She'll always love a part of you and that part will always be the same.

Daniel   I can't see how she'll forgive me.

Cathy   You have to be yourself, Daniel, you can't choose any longer.

Daniel   I'm so scared.

Cathy   I know you are. But I'll be there for you, I promise I will.

Daniel   But your boyfriend could disapprove.

Cathy   I choose my own friends.

Daniel   I'd marry you if you were a man.

They both laugh.

Cathy   Have you always been secretly attracted to men?

Daniel   This is why it's so strange. I never wanted to dress up in girls' clothes when I was a boy. I never had crushes on other boys or on male teachers. What's happened to me – I had no warning of it. It just, all of a sudden, was clear to me one day that I was living a lie. I looked in the mirror and, behind the sadness of the man looking out at me, I saw a woman struggling to get out. And not a very pretty one at that.

Cathy   But this is why you can't blame yourself, Daniel – you were ambushed by your own nature.

Daniel   But it's so unfair. I don't care about myself, but poor Kay – what about her? It's going to be so humiliating for her.

Cathy   It will be for the best.

Daniel   God, you're wonderful. A complete stranger who becomes my new best friend.

Cathy   I'm grateful for it.

Daniel   Why?

Cathy   I feel so close to you, so trusted by you. I feel . . . important.

Daniel   You are important.

Cathy   Can I ask you something? Now that you're becoming a woman . . .

Daniel   But I've such a long way to go.

Cathy   But now that you've started that process . . . the changes you're going through – does it mean that you're no longer attracted to women, that you've suddenly found yourself attracted to men?

Daniel   You know, I've been wondering about this. I think what it is . . . that yes, my true nature is as a woman. But I don't know, it remains to be seen – but the way I feel at the moment, I think I'm probably a lesbian.

Cathy   Really?

Daniel   I want to become a woman, yes, but I don't feel in the least attracted to men, at least not yet. But it wouldn't surprise me if this was just more denial. I don't trust my own nature at present – I mean, I can't because so much of me is changing so quickly. So even though I'm more attracted to women than ever, I suspect it's just a phase – the death throes of my heterosexual manhood.

Cathy   But just because you're destined to be a woman, it doesn't mean you're destined to be a heterosexual woman.

Daniel   It's just so confusing. I just have to let it reveal itself, I think. But one thing, Cathy, and this is quite embarrassing . . .

Cathy   Tell me.

Daniel   When I wear skirts and dresses, I just feel so unbelievably horny. And that causes problems, as you can imagine. You're walking down town, thrilled that no one can recognise you, and you get this ferocious erection. Well, unless the skirt is made of strong material, you're really going to give yourself away.

Cathy   Oh God . . .

Daniel   And this is terrible – a terrible thing to admit. But when I'm in that state the only thing I can do about it . . . I end up ducking into pubs or coffee shops, going into the bathroom and . . .

Cathy   Having a wank?

Daniel   I haven't wanked so much since I was a teenager.

They both laugh.

But I feel so grubby about it. I really feel ashamed.

Cathy   But when you're doing it, who are you fantasising about – men or women?

Daniel   Like I said, I'm open to the possibility that I'm a lesbian.

Cathy   So you think about women?

Daniel   That may change.

Cathy   Who do you think about? Your wife?

Daniel   I know I should . . .

Cathy   But who?

Daniel *is too ashamed to say. He turns away.* **Cathy** *turns his face to hers. She kisses him. Their kissing grows passionate. They start to undress each other, unable to control their hunger.* **Cathy** *puts her head up* **Daniel***'s skirt and begins to suck him off.* **Daniel** *moans, then pushes* **Cathy** *onto the bed, and puts his head up her skirt and begins to lick her out. She moans, then struggles to get up and give pleasure to him, but he pins her there and she comes within minutes, moaning ecstatically. He rises and kisses her. They lie beside each other, one as startled as the other.* **Cathy** *eventually speaks.*

Cathy   I think I'm a lesbian too . . .

Scene Seven

Later that night. **Paul** *is in bed, reading. He's feeling horny.* **Cathy** *enters in her nightdress and gets into bed. Her hair is damp after a shower. He puts his book down. She picks her book up.*

Paul   You took a while.

Cathy   Did I?

Paul   Hot and sweaty?

Cathy   What?

Paul   The shower . . .

Cathy   Yeah. Vacuuming always does that to me . . . Not that I ever really vacuum. Cleaning, though. I think you always feel the need to clean yourself.

Paul   Well, the place is nice and clean now.

Cathy   I was going to leave it to the weekend.

Paul   I was going to do it.

Cathy   You always do it.

Paul   You always do the ironing.

Cathy   Don't worry – I'm not going to ask you to do the ironing.

Paul   Why did you do the vacuuming?

Cathy   The place needed it, that's all. I don't know. Sometimes you do things and you don't know why you did them. Don't you?

Paul   Me?

Cathy   One. It's – maybe it's your unconscious or something, I don't know.

Paul   So, a desire for cleanliness?

Cathy   Maybe.

Paul   For order?

Cathy   You're very awake for this time of night.

Paul   Indeed.

Cathy   What about your book?

He throws it across the room. He looks at her intently.

What did you do that for?

He shrugs.

Why are you looking at me like that?

Paul   Why do you think?

Cathy   Have I got shampoo in my ears?

Paul   No.

Cathy   You're making me uncomfortable.

Paul   Then allow me to make you comfortable.

He ducks under the covers.

Cathy   Paul? Paul, where are you going?

Paul   Don't worry about where I'm going. It's where you're going that matters.

Cathy   And where is that exactly?

He climbs between her legs.

Paul   On a voyage of transcendence . . .

He pulls her knickers down, snaps her legs apart and puts his head between them.

Cathy   Paul, there's no need.

He starts licking her genitals.

Paul, please! I'm too tired, Paul.

He suddenly emerges for air, coughing, his nose powdered white.

Paul (*coughing*)   Jesus Christ.

Cathy   I tried to warn you.

Paul   What the hell?

Cathy   It's talcum powder.

Paul   What's it doing on your cunt?

Cathy   Don't call it that. Only I get to call it that.

Paul   This is no time for feminism, Cathy. Fucking hell.

Cathy   I put some on after my shower.

Paul   Why?

Cathy   Why do you think? I like it.

Paul   But you never use talc. I'm the one that uses talc.

Cathy   Yes, well, now you know my little secret, don't you?

Paul   I could have choked down there. (*Laughs.*)

Cathy   Stop it. You're embarrassing me.

Paul   Where's that glass of water?

He reaches for the glass of water beside the bed and takes a drink, gargles, grins.

I'm not giving up, you know.

Cathy   It's alright.

Paul   How can it be alright? Remember what we spoke about?

Cathy   Of course I remember.

Paul   Well then. I'm making an effort.

Cathy   But why? Why now?

Paul   What does it matter why now? Why not? The same reason you felt the need to clean the house.

Cathy   But I'm . . . I'm fine.

Paul   Fine?

Cathy   I . . . I don't feel very much in the mood, I suppose.

Paul   That's why I'm going to get you in the mood.

Cathy   Paul –

Paul   I won't take no for an answer.

He goes back under.

Cathy (*in desperation*)   I'm having my period!

Paul   So that's what tastes so good.

Cathy (*disgusted*)   Oh for God's sake, get off me.

He does as he's told. She gets out of bed. Silence.

Paul   I was only joking . . . You're not, are you?

Cathy   I'm just not in the mood, alright?

Paul   Alright.

Cathy   Why aren't you tired?

Paul   Do you want me to be tired?

Cathy   You usually are.

Paul   Sometimes I'm not.

Cathy   Can we do it another night?

Paul   No.

Cathy   You're insisting on going down on me?

Paul   I'm being commanding.

Cathy   I don't want you to be commanding.

Paul   This is making me really hard.

Cathy   What is?

Paul   Your resistance. It's great. We should have thought of this before. I've never had such a boner in my life. Come on, Cathy, you want to fuck, don't you? Let's fuck.

Cathy   I don't want to fuck.

Paul   Say it again.

Cathy   I don't want to fuck.

Paul   And again.

Cathy   Paul, I mean it.

Paul   You don't have any choice. I'm stronger than you. I'm going to drag you into bed. I'm going to pull your legs apart and lick you out. And you're going to come like you've never come before.

Resigned, **Cathy** *climbs back into bed.*

Cathy   Oh, go on then.

Paul   What?

Cathy   I'm not going to argue with you.

Paul   Oh, come on.

Cathy   No. If you want to do it, do it.

Paul   But this isn't turning me on.

Cathy   I thought you wanted to turn *me* on?

Paul   I want to turn both of us on.

Cathy   Maybe once you get started I'll join in.

Paul   Okay.

He goes back under the covers and between her legs. He emerges after a few seconds.

Why aren't you . . . I don't understand why you don't appreciate this.

Cathy   I do appreciate it. Sometimes a woman isn't in the mood. How many times –

Paul   In light of recent circumstances that just doesn't add up.

Cathy   I'm tired.

Paul   Neither does that.

Cathy   I can't explain it.

Paul   Neither does that.

Pause. She gets out of bed. She starts to comb her hair. She looks at the comb, reminded of **Daniel**.

Cathy   Look, Paul, I don't know how to tell you this . . .

Paul   It's because I'm not any good at it, isn't it?

Cathy   What?

Paul   That's the truth.

Cathy   No it isn't.

Paul   That's why I take so long – because I don't do it properly.

Cathy   I don't mind you taking a long time. I enjoy it. You're the one that has a problem with it. It tires you out.

Paul   But if I did it the way you want me to do it. If I did it as well as you do it to yourself.

Cathy   But no man can . . . (*She hesitates, realising she's lying.*) You do your best.

Paul   But some men – I bet there are some men who . . . I bet there are. Don't you think?

Cathy   I don't know.

Paul   What I want to know is, how? What makes them better?

Cathy   Practice?

Paul   It's not just that . . .

Cathy   I don't think you like going down on me.

Paul   But that's what I've been trying to do –

Cathy   I know, and it's very sweet of you. But you hardly ever do it. I don't think you enjoy it.

Paul   I don't mind it. I mean . . . I need to feel really aroused, but I don't mind it. I like giving you pleasure.

Cathy   Have you ever actually looked at my genitals?

Paul   I don't need to look. I can find my way with my tongue.

Cathy   Don't you like to look?

Paul   If I'm down there, it means I'm too close to look. I can't see the wood for the . . .

Cathy   For the bush.

Paul   Yeah.

Cathy   But if you knew what to look for, as opposed to thinking you should know when no one's ever actually shown you . . .

Paul   But of course I know what to look for. It's hardly rocket science. Come on, I'll prove it to you.

She shrugs.

Will you let me at least try?

She kisses him. She gets back into bed. He is about to duck down under the covers.

Cathy   Tell me first. What are you looking for?

Paul   What kind of question is that?

Cathy   I'm serious.

Paul   Your . . . your vagina.

Cathy   No.

Paul   No? Your penis?

Cathy   My clitoris.

Paul   Your clitoris, yeah, that's what I meant.

Cathy   Then why didn't you –

Paul   Who cares what it's called? What difference does it make?

Cathy   About an hour. At least.

Paul   Look, don't tell me I don't know what I'm doing. I know what I'm doing.

Cathy   Then tell me this. Where exactly is my clitoris?

Paul   Cathy, the more you treat this like a science class, the less horny I'm getting.

Cathy *shrugs, resignedly.*

Cathy   Good luck.

She lies back, closes her eyes. He goes under the covers again, starts working away. Lights down.

Scene Eight

Lights up. About half an hour has passed. **Paul** *is still at it.* **Cathy** *is fast asleep.*

Paul   Cathy?

She doesn't stir. He climbs out of bed, careful not to wake her. He sits on the edge of the bed. He looks at her, fast asleep.

Cathy!

She doesn't stir. He leaves the room. He returns with a torch. He goes under the covers, between her legs. He turns off the sidelight. He turns on the torch. We see it alight under the covers. Lights down.

Scene Nine

The law firm where **Paul** *and* **Kay** *work.* **Daniel** *is working on* **Paul**'s *laptop. Silence as* **Daniel** *works.* **Paul** *racks his brains for a way to break the ice.*

Paul   So, any idea why it's so slow?

Daniel   Did you notice it slowing down after you installed the anti-virus software?

Paul   Shouldn't that speed it up?

Daniel   Well, it should protect it, but it's heavy on memory, so that might be what's causing it. I'll see if it'll take more RAM.

Pause as **Daniel** *works.*

Paul   We're so used to everything being so fast these days, aren't we? We expect instant results. Impatient.

Daniel   Well, there's no reason your computer shouldn't be fast *and* well protected. It's just a matter of the right hardware and software.

Paul   Speed is important, alright. But it's no good being fast – well, no . . . it's not possible to be fast if you're not doing it right, is it?

Daniel   Not doing it right?

Paul   It. If it's not doing what it's – what you want it to do. Say your computer is supposed to do something, a certain task, like a, like a, like making a connection to a particular site, and say it has all the power in the world – all the willingness to get it right, but it just can't, you know, get there. It's trying and it's trying, but it's just not getting anywhere. And that site – that site that's really important to you – it's just being neglected.

Daniel   Well, what you're talking about could have something to do with the actual internet connection.

Paul   Yes, the connection. I'm not connecting.

Daniel   But there's no problem with the connection.

Paul   What?

Daniel   On your laptop.

Paul   No.

Daniel   Maybe you have the wrong address? The wrong website address.

Paul   Well, that *was* a problem, to be honest. I was looking in the wrong place.

Daniel   Well, it's easy to get that wrong. One digit and you're out.

Paul   You can be an inch away and it might as well be a mile.

Daniel   Do you have the right address now?

Paul   Yes, but there's something else I'm not . . . I mean, I know where to look now, I've got the power, the determination, but I still feel like I can't get in.

Daniel   Maybe you're not allowed access?

Paul   Yeah, that's what it feels like. Like I'm not wanted.

Daniel   I know that feeling.

Paul Yeah?

Daniel Yeah.

Pause as they both reflect on this.

Of course some sites are subscription only.

Paul No, I don't have to pay for it. (*Pause.*) But I know what you mean.

Daniel If you want to tell me what you're looking for, I'm quite good at finding sites, especially tricky ones.

Paul Yeah?

Daniel Well, it's part of my job.

Paul And I bet you're pretty fast?

Daniel Well . . .

Paul What makes you fast, do you think?

Daniel (*puzzled*) Experience, I suppose . . .

Paul Yes, of course, of course.

Daniel Do you want me to look?

Paul No, it's okay, thanks. It's kind of a private thing.

Daniel Oh.

Paul What? Oh God no. You think –

Daniel No, I don't think anything.

Paul It's just a – it's just a football site.

Daniel Okay.

Paul No, the reason – you see, the reason I don't feel welcome is that – well, it's, it's like you do a trial and if you don't do well, you've kind of blown it.

Daniel They don't let you back in?

Paul Yeah. Sort of. Well, they do, but you just don't feel like you've earned your place.

Daniel   I suppose you just have to keep trying.

Paul   Yeah.

Daniel *resumes working on* **Paul***'s laptop.*

Scene Ten

Fintan's coffee shop. **Kay** *and* **Angela** *sit at a table.* **Kay** *enjoys a variety of delicious-looking cakes – eclairs, macaroons, meringues – during the following.*

Kay   God, these macaroons . . .

Angela   How you can even think about food . . . ?

Kay   What else have I got? I'm trying to fill the void he created. Thank God for this place.

Angela   You're unbelievable.

Kay   I'm hungry.

Angela   And what about Daniel? What do you think he is? Laughing behind your back.

Kay   I haven't found the moment.

Angela   You find plenty of time to eat.

Kay   We're having coffee.

Angela   One of us is.

Kay   What's wrong with you? You're the one that wanted to meet.

Angela   You're in denial.

Kay   It's not easy, you know. It's not as simple as going up to him and accusing him of –

Angela   But yes, it is. That's my point.

Kay   You want me to leave him?

Angela   I want you to confront him.

Kay   I'm not ready to.

Angela   Why?

Kay   I'm married, Angela. This is the kind of information that destroys marriages.

Angela   He's the one that destroyed it.

Kay   Maybe he's not having an affair. Maybe he bought the clothes for his mother.

Angela   His mother's dead.

Kay   Maybe he forgot. He was very close to her, you know.

Angela   So this is your coping mechanism? Eat and get fat.

Kay   This has got nothing to do with Daniel. I always eat cake when we meet for coffee. So do you. Usually.

Angela   I'm not hungry.

Kay   Why not?

Angela   I'm really upset about this, you know. I care about you very deeply.

Kay   I know you do.

Angela   Yours was the one marriage that gave me hope.

Kay   Then let's pretend ignorance.

Angela   How can you live like that?

Kay   Because I love him and don't want to believe he could be cheating on me.

Angela   It's a good thing you're a lawyer.

Kay   What's that got to do with anything?

Angela   You need to make sure you get the house.

Kay   How far ahead have you planned this?

Angela   If he has any decency, he won't put up a fight.

Kay *pops another macaroon in her mouth.*

Kay   God, even the coffee ones are nice. Fintan says his pastry chef won't tell him the recipe.

Angela   Why won't you take this seriously?

Kay   The passion fruit ones are amazing too. Have you tried the blueberry eclair?

Angela   Why do I waste my time?

Kay   Although I'm not sure about putting something blue in my mouth.

Angela (*rising*)   I'm going.

She starts to leave.

Kay (*suddenly*)   I'm having an affair.

Angela *is shocked.*

Kay   A guy at work.

Pause.

Angela   Since when?

Kay *is silent, ashamed.*

Angela   It's revenge, isn't it? It's to get back at Daniel for what he's doing to you. For God's sake, Kay, you know that's not the answer.

Kay   It started before his.

Angela   What?

Kay   I . . . Yes.

Angela   Why didn't you tell me? You tell me everything.

Kay   I'm telling you now, aren't I?

Angela   This changes everything.

Kay   People have affairs. So what?

Angela   But why? Why you?

Kay   I . . . I don't know.

Angela   I don't understand you, Kay. I don't understand you at all.

She turns and walks towards the exit. **Kay** *feels judged and humiliated. She rises and shouts.*

Kay   Why are you always telling me how to live my life?

Angela   Why do you think?

Kay   What about yours? You haven't had a boyfriend for years. All you've got is that vibrator I gave you for Christmas God knows when. At least I'm married. At least I have a life.

Angela   People are watching.

Kay   All you do is complain about men, but it's obvious that you're lonely. So why don't you get off your arse and do something about it? I'll tell you why. Because you're a coward.

Angela   Thank you for that pearl of wisdom, Kay. I'll treasure it always.

She leaves.

Kay   Angela! Angela!

She sits down miserably. She looks around self-consciously. She stuffs another macaroon in her mouth.

Scene Eleven

Daniel *and* **Cathy** *are in the closing stages of passionate sex. They climax together – noisily. They lie back in bed, she resting on his chest, he with his arm around her.*

Cathy   I wish my boyfriend could meet you.

Daniel   Why?

Cathy   Why do you think? Oh master . . .

Daniel   Stop.

Cathy   It's true.

Daniel   Well, you know why that is, don't you?

Cathy   No.

Daniel   Think about it.

Cathy   I don't want to think about my boyfriend when I'm lying in bed with you.

Daniel   Who brought him up?

Cathy   Thank you.

Daniel   You can't stop.

Cathy   I can try.

Daniel   It's natural. You love him.

Cathy   I'm beginning to wonder about that.

Daniel *sits up, gets out of bed.*

Cathy   Where are you going?

Daniel   Where are we going?

Cathy   Oh, don't start with that.

He starts to remove his make-up with baby wipes.

Daniel   Comparing me with your partner – you're not comparing like with like.

Cathy   I'm not comparing you, but – well, of course I am. For God's sake, Daniel – how does a person show love, I mean really show it, in the most intimate way possible? By making love, yes?

Daniel   No.

Cathy   Yes!

Daniel   Not necessarily.

Cathy   Oh, come on.

Daniel   There are thousands of other ways, little things you can do for your partner. Opening a door for her, making her dinner, letting her choose what to watch on television –

Cathy   Blah, blah, blah.

Daniel   Those things show love.

Cathy   It's not the same thing.

Daniel   You think it's just about lovemaking?

Cathy   It's the defining thing.

Daniel   So if someone is good at it, they love you; if they're bad at it, they don't?

Cathy   Not exactly, but –

Daniel   And you seem to think I'm wonderful at it –

Cathy   You are.

Daniel   Does that mean I'm in love with you?

Cathy   I . . . I don't know.

Pause.

Daniel   Does it not merely mean that I have had the good fortune, for whatever reason, to acquire some skill in that department?

Cathy   But your willingness to acquire that skill – your sensitivity, your generosity – generosity, that's what love is. To love is to give. And when I'm in bed with you –

Daniel   To be a woman is to give.

Cathy   What?

Daniel   You think it's me – you think I'm showing love?

Cathy   I recognise it when I see it.

Daniel   You think I'm in love with you?

Cathy   Well, I'm in love with you.

Daniel   Cathy . . .

Cathy   And you're not with me. Yes. That's how it goes.

She gets out of bed and begins to dress.

Daniel   You know how confused I am right now.

Cathy   I know we can't get enough of each other.

Daniel   I'm going through a transition.

Cathy   I love you, Daniel.

Daniel   But all you know about me, it's just sex.

Cathy   No, it isn't, that's the point. I got to know you first as a woman, as an aspiring woman –

Daniel   But that's what you're confusing. What you think is love is nothing more than a woman, for the first time in her life, expressing her true nature. If I'm as good a lover as you seem to think I am, it's only because I'm showing the attentiveness to you that all women show to each other and to the men in their lives. And that's why your comparison with your partner is so unfair. He is a man. I am a woman.

Cathy   Daniel, you are not a woman.

Daniel   It's one thing being in denial yourself, but when someone else – someone who's supposed to be supporting you –

Cathy   Okay, you're going through a transition, but you're not a woman yet.

Daniel   I have the nature of a woman, that's the point.

Cathy   You can't generalise about women like that.

Daniel   Women are kind –

Cathy   Oh for God's sake –

Daniel   Generous.

Cathy   All of them?

Daniel   A woman's nature is different from a man's.

Cathy   That is just so fucking stupid.

Daniel   Yes, it is stupid.

Cathy   Women aren't better than men, you idiot. Just because you want to become one doesn't mean it's going to make you a better person. But you're in no position to judge, are you? You've got women on the brain. I suppose if you hated us, you couldn't do it. Daniel, your nature is your nature. It is not the nature of a man, it is not the nature of a woman – it is you.

Daniel   It is me becoming a woman, my true nature.

Cathy   I bet you've always been a generous lover?

Daniel   I've always been a liar.

Cathy   But you have, haven't you?

Daniel   I think I . . . because of guilt, maybe – a guilt I couldn't explain until recently – I always did my best to compensate. It was compensation, not generosity.

Cathy   I bet that's not how your wife thought of it.

Daniel   My wife won't touch me, Cathy. She won't touch me because she sensed that I was lying to her. She knows what my true nature is. At some level, she knows.

Cathy   You know what? I don't believe that. I think that's a load of crap.

Daniel *shrugs.*

Cathy   You think women are so intuitive, don't you? So superior in nature that your wife – just think about this for a minute. You're gently flicking your tongue around her clitoris, she's moaning like a – like an I don't know what – and she's lying there, thinking, you know, there's something insincere about this, this isn't his true nature, actually he must be a woman.

Daniel   She doesn't know I'm a woman. How could she – I didn't know I was one myself.

Cathy   You're not one yourself.

Daniel   Stop saying that. Stop undermining . . . Stop saying that.

Cathy   What I'm saying, Daniel . . . what I'm saying is that it wouldn't surprise me in the least if you're giving her way too much credit. I just don't understand – it doesn't make sense to me that a woman, getting the kind of love she gets from you . . . I just don't understand how she could turn away from you.

Daniel   Because she wasn't getting the kind of love you've been getting from me. The kind of love you're getting from me you're getting because –

Cathy   You're not a fucking woman.

He is terribly hurt. He starts to dress.

Daniel, I'm sorry . . . I just . . . I just – as a woman –

Daniel   Six years of it, Cathy. She's had six years of it. How long have we had? How can you claim to know me as well as she does?

Cathy   You worship women because you want to become one. You think we're kind and generous. Intuitive. I don't think your wife's that intuitive. I don't think she's that generous either. She's the one that's been cold and distant. Did it ever occur to you that the problem could be her?

Daniel   This isn't helping, you know.

Cathy   Why are you so certain it's your fault?

Daniel   Why do you think? Because I'm becoming a woman.

Cathy   Maybe she's making you think you should become a woman.

Daniel   That's ridiculous.

Cathy   Why?

Daniel   Because what's going on . . . I could see in her, it was a kind of growing contempt, an anger, as if she saw through me for the first time, and I felt so guilty –

Cathy   You blamed yourself. Why?

Daniel   I don't know. But when I started thinking about it –
you see, when she saw through me, it made me start looking
at myself and wondering about myself . . . what I could have
done – I could have started an affair with another woman.
Instead, I realised that it wasn't about a lack of sexual
gratification. It was about something much deeper.

Cathy   Daniel, I hate to break it to you, but starting an affair
with another woman is exactly what you've done.

Daniel   I know. And I'm sorry.

Cathy   I'm not . . . When did you last have sex with her?

Daniel   It's been a while.

Cathy   You kept trying?

Daniel   You can't force yourself on someone.

Cathy   So she's the one that called a halt to it?

Daniel   Yes.

Cathy   But why . . . When did you start thinking you were a
woman? What was the moment?

Daniel   I don't know.

Cathy   You'd never thought of it before. You never dressed up
when you were a teenage boy, you never fancied other men –
you still don't.

Daniel   That could be more denial, I don't know.

Cathy   What was the moment?

Daniel   Why does there have to be a moment?

Cathy   Women's intuition.

Daniel   I was . . . this is embarrassing.

Cathy   It's important.

Daniel   Why?

Cathy   Just tell me.

Daniel   I was . . . I was bringing clothes upstairs to put away,
I'd done the ironing. I came across this black skirt of hers, this
short black skirt. I sort of held it for a moment, looking at it.
I don't know why, but – maybe it's because the thought of her
in it, it always turned me on – but I got the urge to try it on.
So I took off my trousers and . . .

Cathy   Did it fit you?

Daniel   Yes, it did. I zipped it up at the side. There was a
button.

Cathy   How did it make you feel?

Daniel   Very, very aroused. But then I went to look at myself
in the mirror. I was convinced I'd look as sexy as hell. I looked
terrible, really unattractive. And it bothered me. I realised I
wanted to look attractive. I also realised that these were the
clothes for me. Skirts, silk panties, stockings . . . I wanted to
feel sexy. I wanted to look sexy.

Cathy   Since we've started sleeping together, have you felt
the same urge to dress up as a woman?

Daniel   I love being undressed as a woman. I love it when
you remove my wig, wipe away my make-up. I love it when
you put your hands up my skirt and feel my arse and push that
silk against me. I love it when you go on your knees and put
your head up my skirt and suck me. I love it when you pull my
skirt off and my knickers and my stockings. I even love it when
you pull the socks out of my bra, one by one.

Cathy   I love it when you're naked. I love it when you're a
man again.

Daniel   But you like me in women's clothes?

Cathy   I like you in any clothes. I like you out of any clothes.

Daniel   But as a woman, I . . . You find me attractive, don't
you?

Cathy   I find you attractive as a man dressed up as a woman.

Daniel   Yes, but you're heterosexual.

Cathy So are you.

Daniel I'm a lesbian.

Cathy Then so am I.

Daniel You're attracted to men.

Cathy You are a man.

Daniel I'm becoming a woman.

Cathy You dress like a woman.

Daniel I am going through a change.

Cathy If you're in denial about anything, it's your manhood.

Daniel I dressed up in my wife's skirt.

Cathy And you got an erection.

Daniel Well, I won't be getting those forever.

Cathy What?

Daniel I want to become a woman, Cathy.

Cathy You're not going to . . . Daniel . . . ?

Daniel My wife has given me six years of her life. If I'm going to end it, I want to stand before her as a woman so that she knows . . . I want to set her free.

Cathy Then divorce her. Leave her. You don't have to cut your dick off to set her free.

Daniel I need her to understand. I need her to see that it's not her fault. I can't forgive myself for depriving her of the opportunity for children.

Cathy If she wants children, she should let you –

Daniel I want to give her freedom.

Cathy But Daniel, you . . . you love making love, you . . . you can't give that up.

Daniel   I don't intend to. I just intend to do it as a woman in the future.

Cathy   But what if you . . . what if you realise it was all a terrible mistake?

Daniel   I won't. Men have intuition too, Cathy, especially when they're women. I know what I'm doing.

Scene Twelve

Daniel *and* **Kay** *in bed, reading magazines. He looks at her for a long time. So much to tell her if only he could. He returns to his magazine. She looks at him for a long time. So much to tell him if only she could.*

Scene Thirteen

Paul *is in bed, waiting for* **Kay**. *He checks his watch. He picks up his mobile phone.* **Kay** *enters, carrying two paper bags.*

Kay   Sorry I'm late.

Paul   What took you?

Kay   Are you hungry?

Paul   Not for food.

Kay   No, we're going to get it right this time. We're going to eat first and then, you know . . .

Paul   I don't want to eat first. I want to –

Kay   No way, if you want my full attention you're going to have to let me eat.

Paul   Well, can we at least eat off each other?

Kay   No, I don't think so. I don't want chicken tikka all over the sheets.

Paul   Who cares about the sheets? We're in a hotel.

Kay   Even so. Do you eat chicken tikka?

He shakes his head in dismay. She hands him a bag and sits on the bed.

How's your day going?

Paul   My day? Kay . . .

Kay   I'm plugging the gaps for Michelle again. She's away for a week and this client – she never told me he'd be in touch, one of hers, and I come in this morning and he's sitting there, ready for a meeting he apparently scheduled through Michelle –

Paul   We're not here to talk about work. We're not here to have lunch.

Kay   It's natural to talk about work, especially when we work in the same place. And we have to have lunch – we have to eat.

Paul   Get undressed.

Kay   I'm eating my sandwich.

Paul   Get undressed, Kay.

Kay   I'm eating my sandwich first.

Paul   What is it about you and food?

Kay   These sugar lows – I've told you before. Do you really want me lying there thinking about my lunch?

Paul   No, I want you thinking about me. Not food, not Michelle's clients. Now please take off your clothes.

Kay   I will. Just let me eat first.

Paul   What have you got? Chicken tikka – what else?

Kay   Not much. A yogurt and some fruit. A KitKat, which I'm going to have with a nice cup of tea. I'd better put the kettle on, actually.

She goes to put the kettle on.

Paul   And you intend to consume all that before getting into bed with me?

Kay   Yes. And I recommend that you do the same.

Paul   Are you aware that you're a slow eater?

Kay   I was always taught to chew my food before swallowing it. For digestion.

Paul   So basically we're going to have fuck-all time for sex?

Kay   It's not my fault our lunch hour is so short.

Paul   But you're okay with that?

Kay   We'll still have a few minutes. Look, I can toss you off while I'm eating if you want.

Paul   I can do that myself.

Kay   While you're eating? Wow, I'd like to see that. (*She laughs.*) Sorry.

He shakes in head in frustration. He moves towards her. She puts her sandwich behind her back.

You've got yours. Leave mine alone.

He starts unbuttoning her blouse.

Stop it.

She moves away. He follows her.

Paul . . .

Paul   Does this turn you on?

Kay   No . . .

Paul   Yes it does . . .

Kay   Just let me eat my –

He knocks the sandwich out of her hand.

I'll eat yours then.

He advances and lifts up her skirt. She tries to pull it down, but he's stronger.

Stop it.

Paul   I'm going to fuck you.

He tries to pull down her knickers, but realises she's wearing tights.

Why aren't you wearing stockings? You're supposed to be wearing stockings.

Kay   Let go of me . . . Because it's cold.

He pulls down her tights.

Paul   I'm going to give you the orgasm of a lifetime.

He tries to pull down her knickers, but she kicks him hard between the legs. He doubles over, in agony. She pulls up her tights and straightens her skirt. She steps over him and kneels down to pick up her lunch from the floor.

What did you do that for?

Kay   It was either that or scream.

Paul   I was trying to turn you on.

Kay   Well, you've got a funny way of going about it.

Paul   Well, you've got a funny way of carrying on an affair. You don't have any interest in this, do you?

Kay   Yes, I do.

Paul   You don't fancy me in the least.

Kay   Of course I do.

Paul   Kay, you'd rather eat lunch.

She is silent, knowing this is true.

I know I've . . . I know I haven't been great in bed –

Kay   You've been . . . That isn't the problem.

Paul   Compared to what you're used to –

Kay   You've been lovely.

Paul   But I'm going to improve. I just need you to give me a chance. I've done a bit of research and I know what to do. Your husband set the standard and I want to –

Kay   But I don't want you to be like him, don't you see? I thought you understood that I just wanted to be fucked.

Paul   But that's not what I want.

Kay   You want me to come. God Almighty, I thought you were old-fashioned. Why can't you just be old-fashioned? I hate feminism. It's destroyed everything. Don't you see, Paul? I wanted a *man*.

Paul   You don't think I'm a man?

Kay   Of course you are, but . . . My husband is a great lover, but . . . it's just not enough. There's something missing.

Paul   Maybe it's to do with the man. Maybe if I'm a great lover, there won't be something missing.

Kay   But what would that mean? . . . Do you mean you want us to fall in love?

Paul   No. I mean I want us to enjoy having sex together, that's all. I don't think we can hope for any more. Do you?

Kay   No, I suppose not.

Paul   But that's not what you want, is it?

Kay   Oh, I don't know what I want. Apart from food all the time.

Paul   I'm . . . I'm learning, I'm improving. It's not that I've been practising, but there's something I want to try. I want to try it on you.

Kay   You want to practise on me?

Paul   Yes.

Kay   Why don't you practise on your girlfriend?

Paul   My girlfriend doesn't want to have sex with me. I don't blame her. I haven't . . . I've let her down. I want to practise and improve and then . . .

Kay   You want to unleash yourself on her?

Paul   I want to win her back.

Kay   So you just want to use me, that's what you're saying?

Paul   I was sort of hoping you might enjoy the prospect.

Kay   There's no future for us, is there?

Paul   But there never was. We don't love each other.

Kay   No.

Paul   You love your husband, I love my girlfriend.

Kay   Do we? I don't think I want to stay with my husband.

Paul   What do you want then? You don't want to be with me.

Kay   Of course not.

Paul   Then what's this for?

Kay   Sex.

Paul   But how can it be for sex if you don't want . . . ?

Kay   I do want to . . . Well, I did want to.

Paul   Until you did it.

Kay   No, no.

Paul   Oh come on. All this stuff about food – it's just a way of avoiding something you don't enjoy, or don't enjoy with me.

Kay   But that isn't true, Paul. It's refreshing, believe it or not – at least you're different from Daniel.

Paul   You mean worse.

Kay   But I want you to be worse. That's my point. I just feel so damn guilty when he's . . . I just don't feel worthy of it.

Paul   But when I've got my head between your legs and I'm getting nowhere – you feel worthy of that?

Kay   I'm sorry. I just feel I'm getting all I deserve.

Paul   Thanks, Kay.

Kay   Sorry. But that's not what I want either, I've tried to tell you. I want to be fucked. Fucked, not loved. I'm sick of being loved. It's killing me.

Paul   It's all a mystery, if you ask me.

Kay   Tell me about it.

Paul   What are you going to do?

Kay   I think we should put a stop to these lunches. They're satisfying neither of us.

Paul   I agree.

Kay   I'm sorry, Paul, I really don't know what I'm looking for. I thought it was sex, but of course it isn't. I thought it was a change, but . . .

Paul   Are you going to have an affair with someone else now?

Kay   Why would I want to do that?

Paul   Well, so that you might find whatever you're looking for.

Kay   But what am I looking for?

Paul   The right kind of lunch?

Kay   Do you mind if I eat your sandwich?

Paul   It's all yours.

He starts to dress. Miserably, she starts to eat the sandwich.

Scene Fourteen

The law firm where **Paul** *and* **Kay** *work.* **Daniel** *is working on* **Paul***'s laptop. Silence as* **Daniel** *works.*

Paul   Thanks for having another look. I don't know what's wrong with it.

Daniel   The RAM should have done the trick. The anti-virus software might have to go after all.

Paul   Well, it is faster. It's just, you know, not as fast as I'd like.

Daniel   Presumably you weren't able to access that site?

Paul   Sorry?

Daniel   The football one. The one that didn't want to let you in.

Paul   Yeah. Not much progress, I'm afraid.

Daniel   All the more reason to achieve maximum performance.

Daniel *works away in silence. Once again,* **Paul** *searches for a clever way to raise his topic. He gives up.*

Paul   Daniel, can I ask you something?

Daniel   Sure.

Paul   Something that's got nothing to do with computers.

Daniel   Okay . . .

Paul   Let me see . . . How should I put this? . . . I mean, what do you think about women, Daniel?

Daniel   Women?

Paul   Look, I know you're fixing my computer, but, you know, we're men, when do we get to talk about these things?

Daniel   I . . . I don't know.

Paul   That's my point. It just doesn't happen. Except when men are fixing things together. And here we are fixing something together, discussing RAM and memory and – you know . . . So I think that means we can talk.

Daniel   I don't want to disrupt your day. I know you're busy.

Paul   It's okay with me if it's okay with you . . .

Daniel   Okay . . .

Paul   Do you think . . . okay, let me ask you – do you mind me asking you?

Daniel I don't know. Asking me what?

Paul Biologically, if we accept that God created men and women, or whoever created them, but if we can just say it's God for the sake of simplicity . . . can we?

Daniel Okay.

Paul Well, do you think he did a good job? Do you think he got it right, in other words?

Daniel About men or women?

Paul Both.

Daniel I think he got women right . . .

Paul Yeah?

Daniel I think women are the most beautiful, most wondrous, most extraordinary creatures imaginable.

Paul Go on.

Daniel I think they're so superior to men as to render questionable the whole question of a creator. Because what creator, except perhaps for a sick joke, could get one thing so exquisitely right and the other so monumentally wrong? (*Pause.*) Sorry. No offence.

Paul None taken. (*Pause.*) Are you married? Do you mind me asking?

Daniel Yes. I mean, no. I am married. In fact my wife works –

Paul Well, anyway, I'm just asking generally, and don't get me wrong, I'm sure she's a wonderful person and –

Daniel She is.

Paul Okay, okay. But doesn't she – there must be days, occasions, where she rubs you up the wrong way, and it's not because she's – it's not because of her personality as such, it's because she's a woman?

Daniel Right.

Paul   Sorry, that was a question.

Daniel   Oh. Well. Let me see . . .

He thinks for a very long time.

Sorry, the answer is no.

Paul   No?

Daniel   There is nothing about the fact that she's a woman that annoys me. The fact that she's a woman constitutes about ninety per cent of the things I adore about her. The other ten per cent she provides herself in the form of personality, love, support, intelligence, beauty, imagination, character –

Paul   Okay.

Daniel   Was there something specific you wanted to ask?

Paul   Look, when it comes to sex, we're hunters, right? We see a good-looking woman, we want to have sex with her, don't we? I'm not saying we have sex with her, but we want to – yeah?

Daniel   That can happen, yes.

Paul   But in the way that we, say, want to shag her, we don't necessarily picture ourselves making love to her, with candles and, you know, tenderness or whatever – we sort of want to just do it, don't we? We want to just shag and then go and have something to eat, don't we? And I don't mean something vegetarian, I mean something bloody. I mean, this whole idea of making love, of making love as opposed to shagging, is that something that Jane Eyre came up with, or one of those female novelists? Is that something that's intrinsic to the way men and women instinctively do things or is it something that some woman invented and then persuaded other women they should expect and then made men feel they should do? Even though it's not in our nature?

Daniel   But I think it is in our nature. I think what's not in our nature is the idea that we should just take. I think we, as men, are ashamed to believe that it's okay to savour a woman's body. And I mean savour in the sense of worship, of physically worship.

Paul   You're talking about cunnilingus, aren't you? Oral?

Daniel   Among other things.

Paul   Why – what else is there?

Daniel   Well . . .

Paul   But you're big into going down?

Daniel   I'd live down there if I could.

Paul   Wow.

Daniel   I don't think early man thought so little of woman that he just wanted to take from her. I think he was closer to nature than we are, I think he saw her as a creation of nature and wanted to treasure her.

Paul   You think cavemen were into cunnilingus?

Daniel   Yes. Yes, I do. I think the cavemen of prehistoric times were much more enlightened in their attitudes to women than the actual cavemen of today.

Paul   Right. Is there any scientific evidence about that?

Daniel   It's just a personal theory. It may have no basis in fact.

Paul   Okay . . . If a caveman was good at . . . if he was a good lover back in the day and say he was going back to his cave after a good day's hunting, and say his woman had cooked his dinosaur steak for him and he was in good form and wanted to thank her . . . how long do you think it would've taken him to put a big smile on her lips, if you know what I mean?

Daniel   Surely it would have depended on the caveman. And woman.

Paul   Just roughly, I mean.

Daniel   I don't know. Are you asking me how long it takes me to give my wife an orgasm?

Paul   Am I?

Daniel   I think you are.

Paul   I don't think I have the right to ask you such a personal question.

Daniel   Do you have a wife?

Paul   Girlfriend.

Daniel   Do you go down on her?

Paul   That's a very personal question. (*Pause.*) Actually, I go down on her all the time.

Daniel   And do you think it matters how long it takes when you're giving her pleasure? Do you not think, in a way, that the longer it takes, the better?

Paul   I guess my question is, what makes a caveman good at it? What's his secret, in other words?

Pause as **Daniel** *considers this.*

Daniel   Purity of heart.

Paul   Purity of . . . ? But what about technique? And knowledge – knowing where, you know, his tongue should go?

Daniel   But technique can be learned and knowledge can be gained.

Paul   But what about determination? Never giving up?

Daniel   I think sometimes you have to let go if that's what she wants. If the caveman and woman truly love each other and can talk to each other . . . Do you love your girlfriend?

Paul   Yeah, I do.

Daniel   Can you talk to her about this kind of thing?

Paul   I think so.

Daniel   Then who cares about speed? What's the rush?

Paul   I suppose.

Daniel   I envy you.

Paul   Really?

Daniel *nods. Pause.* **Daniel** *resumes working on* **Paul***'s laptop.* **Paul** *smiles to himself, pleased at the idea that he is envied.*

Paul   I'll tell you one thing, Daniel. For a guy that fixes computers, you're pretty damn interesting.

Daniel   I think I appreciate women, that's all. And I think that makes me a very lucky man.

Paul   I feel equally blessed. We should form a club. The women-worshippers.

Daniel   And I've got some good news for you. You don't have to change your anti-virus software to speed up your laptop.

Paul   Oh no?

Daniel   All you have to do is delete some of your porn.

Scene Fifteen

Cathy *waits anxiously in Fintan's coffee shop.* **Kay** *enters.*

Cathy   Kay?

Kay   Yes.

Cathy   Cathy. (*They shake hands.*) Thanks for meeting me here.

Kay   That's quite alright. Our meeting rooms are very stuffy, formal.

Cathy   Would you like something to eat?

Kay   Yes, absolutely. (*Picks up the menu.*) This place does great takeaway lunches. I think I'll have the goat's cheese, chorizo and sun-dried tomato sandwich – with avocado and chopped olives. What are you having?

Cathy   I'm not hungry, thanks.

Kay   Are you sure? Not even a coffee and some macaroons? I can never understand people who aren't hungry. I hate those films where people order food and then don't eat it. I want to dive through the screen and snatch it off their plates!

Cathy   Yes, I know what you mean. I'll get something later. (*Unsure how to begin this.*) Thanks for meeting me.

Kay   Sorry, I'm forgetting myself. Maybe that's why you're not hungry. You said something on the phone about your employer – it's an unfair dismissal case you're interested in pursuing?

Cathy   Yes, I . . . I got into trouble for serving a customer.

Kay   You work in a woman's shop, don't you?

Cathy   The lingerie department of Fitzhenry's. Do you know it?

Kay   Yes, I do. They do very sexy underwear.

Cathy   The customer I got into trouble for serving . . . it was a man.

Pause. **Kay** *looks more closely at* **Cathy**, *beginning to recognise her.*

Kay   What kind of man?

Cathy   Your husband.

Kay   I'm sorry, I should have recognised you immediately.

Cathy   It's okay. I didn't want to make it awkward for you.

Kay   Thanks for . . . thanks for the ruse. But they haven't fired you for that, have they?

Cathy   No. And that's not why I wanted to meet you. Your husband isn't having an affair. I mean, he didn't buy those clothes for another woman. He bought them for himself.

Kay   What?

Cathy   We've become friends. Daniel and I have become friends. I served him the first time, he came back again after that. He asked me to help him become a woman.

Kay   He wants to . . . he wants to become a woman?

Cathy   Yes . . .

Kay   Are you . . . ? What are you talking about?

Cathy   Look, I know I have no right to know, but he told me a lot of private things about your relationship. He thinks he's been lying to you during all the time you've been together. He thinks the reason it hasn't been going well is that . . . is that his true nature is as a woman.

Kay   Jesus Christ.

Cathy   I'm sorry . . . He thinks you sensed this. Did you?

Kay   What?

Cathy   Is that why you won't let him near you?

Kay   He had no right to tell you – to tell you –

Cathy   Can we get beyond that, please? Do you believe your husband, deep down, to be a woman? Yes or no? I know this is a lot to take in, but this is really important. He's not just dressing up as a woman, he's planning to become one, really become one.

Kay   Daniel as a woman?

Cathy   Does that make some kind of sense?

Kay   Daniel as a woman . . .

Cathy   Is that what you think he is?

Kay   I've no idea. I never thought of him like that before. But now that you mention it . . .

Cathy   But how could you think that?

Kay   I didn't think it. You suggested it. I'm only thinking it now.

Cathy   Well, I don't think it's possible. I think he's got it wrong. Look, Kay, I know what kind of man he is. I shouldn't, but I do.

Kay   I don't understand.

Cathy   I know what a wonderful lover he is.

Kay   You've been sleeping with him?

Cathy   I'm sorry . . .

Kay   Poor Daniel . . .

Cathy   What?

Kay   Do you love him?

Cathy   Do I love him? My point is, I don't think he's a woman.

Kay   But do you love him?

Cathy   You want me to?

Kay   He deserves . . . (*She turns away.*)

Cathy   What does he deserve?

Kay   To be happy, of course. I just want him to be happy.

Cathy   Don't you love him?

Kay   Of course I love him. I'm enormously fond of him. Are you married?

Cathy   I'm in a relationship.

Kay (*disappointed*)   Oh.

Cathy   I thought I loved him – Daniel, I mean. I was wrong, I think. I'm not leaving my boyfriend, if that's what you're asking.

Kay   Poor Daniel . . . And yet I'm so relieved that at least – and you seem so nice. I've been having an affair too, you see. I don't know what I was looking for, but I didn't find it. It wasn't his fault. I don't know what's wrong with me.

Cathy   Well, he thinks there's something wrong with him.

Kay Paul . . . ? I mean Daniel. Sorry, Paul's the man I've been sleeping with.

Cathy My boyfriend's called Paul.

Kay Imagine if they were the same Paul. That would be quite a coincidence.

Cathy Yes, it would. I don't know what I'd do if my boyfriend had an affair.

Kay What could you do? You've had one yourself.

Cathy I know. But Daniel and I didn't set out to have one, it just happened.

Kay I know what you mean. But I always think you're responding to some need, don't you?

Cathy I suppose.

Kay Whether it's boredom or dissatisfaction, or the need to be loved or . . . or find something that's missing.

Cathy Why did you have your affair?

Kay It still doesn't make sense to me. I just wanted to try someone different.

Cathy Sexually?

Kay Yes.

Cathy Did you learn anything from it?

Kay Yes. That I'd rather eat a chicken tikka sandwich than have a man go down on me. Isn't that terrible?

Cathy Well, sometimes I'd rather read a book.

Kay Why did you have your affair?

Cathy Daniel just broke my heart. He's terribly unhappy, Kay. He's lonely, he's confused. Do you think it's possible that deep down he really should be a woman?

Kay I don't know. Only he can answer that.

Cathy   But don't you understand what's going on here? He's going to become a woman just for you.

Kay   He's going to have operations and things?

Cathy   That's why I wanted to meet you. If he's on the wrong track, he's got to be stopped.

Kay   I need to see him. I need to see him as a woman. Can you help me?

Cathy *nods.*

Scene Sixteen

Cathy's *bedroom.* **Daniel** *sits on the edge of the bed, dressed more convincingly as a woman than we have seen him before. He is touching up his make-up using a hand mirror.*

Kay *enters, but he has her back to her and is too focused on his make-up to see her.*

Daniel   I was wondering, if it's not too much trouble, if you'd come with me to the doctor. I know I'm going to have a million questions and I'll forget most of them. You've been there from the start and I'd love you to be there right through to . . . you know. I think it would be better if I go dressed like this so that she can see that I'm serious. What do you . . . ?

He has seen **Kay** *in the mirror. He rises and turns away, ashamed.*

Kay   Let me look at you.

Daniel   I'm not ready . . . What are you doing here? . . . She told you, didn't she?

Kay   Let me look at you.

Daniel   I'm sorry.

Kay   Look at me. Please.

He turns to face her. She looks at him, admiring him.

You're so beautiful.

Daniel   Am I?

Kay *approaches him. She strokes his face, his hair. She looks at his breasts. Overcome by desire, she kisses him suddenly and passionately. They pull at each other's clothes and fall onto the bed. She, on top of him, goes under his skirt. He lies back to savour this, but she emerges after a few moments and walks away. He rises, confused. She turns back to him. She approaches him. She unbuttons his blouse, but not seductively, mechanically. When he tries to touch her, she pushes his hands away. She looks at his bra stuffed with socks. She pulls the socks out one by one, until both cups, like* **Daniel***, are deflated. She sits on the bed. He sits beside her. She starts to cry. He puts his arm around her and pulls her gently into his chest. She cries into his chest.*

Daniel   It'll be alright.

Kay   How?

Daniel   When I have the operation, I'll be as I'm meant to be, as you want me to be.

Kay   What?

He is taken aback by her shock. She moves away from him.

Daniel   I saw it in your eyes. You can't deny it. That's how you want me. As a woman.

Kay   No –

Daniel   You can't lie to yourself.

Kay   Stop it! Just stop!

Daniel   I can change.

Kay   How far would you go? Would you die for me?

Daniel   Of course.

Kay   Well, don't. It won't be appreciated, and neither will cutting off your dick. I don't want your dick, I don't want your balls. Keep them.

Pause. He turns away, hurt and rejected.

What is it about you, Daniel? What is it about you that makes you want me so badly?

Daniel   I love you.

Kay   I'm your wife and I don't even know who you are. I don't even know what you want.

Daniel   I want you to be happy.

Kay   But you can't make me happy. Don't you see? I don't want you as a woman. I don't want you as a man. I don't want you at all.

Daniel   Thank you.

Kay   Why do you think you always have to give?

Daniel   It's the one thing I thought I was good at.

She sits back down beside him.

Kay   Oh, Daniel. You're so much better than that. Why do you hate yourself so much?

He is silent.

The more you try to give to me, the more you're giving up of yourself. Why can't you give to yourself?

Daniel   I don't know what to give.

Kay   Yes you do.

She strokes his hair.

Daniel   I don't know what I want, Kay. I never have. Do you?

Kay   I'm scared, Daniel.

Daniel   Me too.

They put their arms around each other, holding each other for support.

Scene Seventeen

Kay *and* **Angela** *are having lunch at Fintan's.* **Kay** *hasn't touched her sandwich.*

Angela   Why aren't you eating? You've got to eat. You've got to keep your strength up.

But **Kay** *just stares at her sandwich.*

Angela   You can't just let him get away with it. He's having sex with this other woman and you're just sitting idly by, being a victim. Is that where feminism got us? Is that what you want to be all your life, Kay – a victim? I'm sorry for being so blunt, but that's what you need – someone to shake you up and spell it out. Snap out of it, Kay. You have to confront him about it.

Kay   You know, I've often wondered why we're friends.

Angela   We're friends because we're there for each other, because we're not afraid to tell each other the truth.

Kay   But we don't tell each other the truth. I tell you what I want to tell you and you try to fix my life.

Angela   That's because your life needs fixing.

Kay   I don't think we are friends, not really. I don't even like you.

Angela   What?

Kay   I'm sorry, Angela. I'm sorry to hurt your feelings.

Angela   Of course you like me.

Kay   Can I show you why I think we spend time together? Can I show you why I think I like to spend time with you?

Angela   What do you mean 'show me'?

Kay   If friends tell each other the truth, well, that's what I want to do. But I want to show you the truth.

Angela   How?

Kay   Just trust me, please. It won't hurt.

Angela   Alright. If you want. Whatever you mean.

Kay   Close your eyes.

Angela   You're not going to slap me, are you?

Kay   No.

Angela   But why do you want me to . . . ?

Kay   Please. Just close your eyes.

Angela *closes her eyes.* **Kay** *rises. She kisses* **Angela** *softly on the mouth, looks at her.* **Angela** *is stunned and speechless.*

Kay   Yeah, that's what it is.

Kay *sits down.* **Angela** *just sits there, stunned.* **Kay** *picks up her sandwich, but puts it down again.* **Kay** *looks at* **Angela** *in the hope that the attraction is mutual. Slowly, tentatively,* **Kay** *moves her hand across the table towards* **Angela***'s. But* **Angela** *moves her hand away.* **Angela** *looks at* **Kay** *and shakes her head.* **Angela** *rises. She takes some change out of her purse and puts it on the table as a tip. She tries to think of something to say, but can't. She leaves.* **Kay** *sits there, alone.*

Scene Eighteen

Paul *is in bed, reading a women's magazine.* **Cathy** *enters in her nightdress, sits on the bed and takes off her make-up.* **Paul** *drops the magazine beside the bed and looks at her admiringly.*

Cathy   What?

Paul   I'm just admiring my lovely girlfriend.

Cathy   Lovely before I remove my make-up or after?

Paul   Both.

Cathy   Why aren't you reading your book?

Paul   What book?

Cathy   You finished it?

Paul   No.

Cathy   Then why aren't you reading?

Paul   Are you getting into bed?

She gets into bed. He continues to stare at her.

Cathy   What's going on? I don't like this, I feel like I must have done something.

Paul   Are you going to read?

Cathy   That's what we do when we go to bed.

Paul   I thought that was under review.

Cathy   Is it?

Paul   Yes. Leaving us free to find other ways to put ourselves to sleep.

Cathy   Well, just because you don't want to read doesn't mean I don't want to.

Paul   Okay then, read.

Cathy   I'd quite like to.

Paul   I'm not stopping you.

Cathy   I find that I look forward to it.

Paul   You can't beat a good book.

He smiles and turns away from her. She looks at him guiltily. She looks as if she may speak to him, but holds back. She reaches down beside her bed to get her book. She can't find it.

Cathy   Have you seen my book?

Paul   Oh. Sorry.

He reaches down beside his side of the bed and retrieves her book and hands it to her.

Cathy   Did you want to read it?

Paul   No, not particularly.

Cathy   You just wanted to look at it?

Paul   No.

Cathy   Then what was it doing on your side of the bed?

Paul   I had this notion . . . I was hiding it so that you'd have no choice but to make love to me.

Cathy   Really?

Paul   Yeah.

Cathy   Why did you change your mind?

Paul   Because I know you don't want to.

Cathy   How can you – ?

Paul   Because that's what it means . . . doesn't it?

Cathy   I . . . I've been enjoying it and . . . it doesn't necessarily –

Paul   It's fine, Cathy, don't feel bad about it.

Cathy   But you can't assume that I don't want to make love to you just because –

Paul   Of course I can. That's exactly what I can assume. Let's be honest about it.

Cathy   I'm just . . . I'm going through something strange at the moment.

Paul   I know. Both of us are. Hiding the book was a stupid idea.

Cathy   Well . . .

Paul   The bottom line is, I haven't been a good lover –

Cathy   You're a wonderful lover –

Paul   No, I'm not. I'm going to try to improve. But I can't force you to . . . I just want you to give me another chance.

Cathy   What do you mean? That sounds so . . . We're not in trouble, are we?

Paul   I just think this is important. I do love you, Cathy, I really do, and I've never had any difficulty saying that. So I'm not going to rush you. I'm going to leave you be until you're ready. You can read as many books as you want and I'll just wait until you're finished. But I'm not going to read in bed any more. It's when I'm in bed that I'm closest to you and it's not just a place to sleep. It's a place to be intimate with you. No book has been written that's good enough to get between me and you. And you know something? Cavemen didn't have books. They spent all night making love to their women. That's the kind of caveman I want to be.

He turns away to sleep. She is very moved.

Cathy   If that was some elaborate come-on, it's working.

Paul   It wasn't. Read your book.

Cathy   Why do I think that making love is the most important way of showing love?

Paul   Well, I suppose it is.

Cathy   But what you're doing, what you've just said, that's the most gorgeous thing I've ever heard.

Paul   Really?

Cathy   Come here.

She hugs him. She rests his head on her chest, stroking his hair.

Paul   So, can I go down on you tonight?

Cathy   No. Tonight I just want to hold you.

Pause.

Paul   Please.

Cathy   That's not all there is to sex, you know.

Paul   Pretty please.

Cathy   Maybe later.

Scene Nineteen

Darkness. The sound of **Cathy** *moaning begins, growing louder and more frantic until she comes. Her heavy breathing gradually subsides.*

Paul (*triumphantly*)   Yes!

They both laugh.

Scene Twenty

Cathy *is working in the shop, dressing a model.* **Daniel** *enters. He is dressed in a suit. He is bereft, confused, relieved, grateful – generally bewildered by what he has gone through.*

Daniel   Hi.

Cathy   Hello . . .

Pause.

Daniel   I cancelled the appointment.

Cathy   Good.

Daniel   Yeah. (*Pause.*) You . . . you really saved me.

Cathy   Never mind about that.

Daniel   I nearly made a bit of a fool of myself. (*Pause.*) I don't know how I can ever thank you.

Cathy   You're welcome. Any time. (*Pause.*) How's Kay?

Daniel   She's moving out.

Pause. He shrugs. As painful as it is, what more is there to say?

Cathy   How are you?

Daniel   I don't know. (*Pause.*) I thought it was all my fault.

Cathy   I know.

Daniel   But it wasn't.

Cathy   No. (*Pause.*) At least you know now. At least, you know, you can move on.

Daniel   Yes. Yes. (*Pause.*) But why did I want to try on a bra?

Cathy   You like wearing women's clothes. Doesn't mean you're a woman.

Daniel   No. It doesn't, does it?

She shakes her head.

I do love wearing women's clothes, I really do.

Cathy   Then you've come to the right place.

Daniel   Really?

Cathy   You're allowed, you know.

Pause. He grins shyly.

Daniel   This is kind of exciting.

Cathy   So it should be.

Pause.

Daniel   Cathy, there's something that I . . . You said you were . . . you said you were in love with me . . .

Cathy   Yes.

Daniel   I just need to . . .

Cathy   Is that a hope or a question?

Daniel   I don't know.

Cathy   I think I want to stay with my boyfriend, Daniel.

Daniel   I'm glad.

Cathy   Are you . . . Are you okay with that?

Daniel   I think what I need is a friend.

Cathy   I'd love it if we could be friends.

Daniel   Just someone to talk to. To talk to about clothes.

Cathy It would be my pleasure.

Pause.

Daniel I should let you get back to work.

Cathy You know where to find me.

He turns away. She watches him go. He turns back to her.

Daniel Cathy?

Cathy Yes?

Daniel I was just wondering, what's new in stock?

Cathy There's some nice underwear. What have you got in mind?

Daniel I don't know. Just so long as it's sexy . . .

Curtain.

Methuen Drama Student Editions

Jean Anouilh *Antigone* • John Arden *Serjeant Musgrave's Dance*
Alan Ayckbourn *Confusions* • Aphra Behn *The Rover*
Edward Bond *Lear* • Bertolt Brecht *The Caucasian Chalk Circle*
Life of Galileo • *Mother Courage and her Children*
The Resistible Rise of Arturo Ui • *The Threepenny Opera*
Anton Chekhov *The Cherry Orchard* • *The Seagull* • *Three Sisters*
Uncle Vanya • Caryl Churchill *Serious Money* • *Top Girls*
Shelagh Delaney *A Taste of Honey* • Euripides *Elektra* • *Medea*
Dario Fo *Accidental Death of an Anarchist* • Michael Frayn *Copenhagen*
John Galsworthy *Strife* • Nikolai Gogol *The Government Inspector*
Robert Holman *Across Oka* • Henrik Ibsen *A Doll's House*
Hedda Gabler • Charlotte Keatley *My Mother Said I Never Should*
Bernard Kops *Dreams of Anne Frank* • Federico García Lorca
Blood Wedding • *The House of Bernarda Alba* (bilingual edition)
Yerma (bilingual edition) • David Mamet *Glengarry Glen Ross*
Oleanna • Patrick Marber *Closer* • Joe Orton *Loot*
Luigi Pirandello *Six Characters in Search of an Author*
Mark Ravenhill *Shopping and F***ing* • Willy Russell *Blood Brothers*
Sophocles *Antigone* • Wole Soyinka *Death and the King's Horseman*
August Strindberg *Miss Julie* • J. M. Synge *The Playboy of the
Western World* • Theatre Workshop *Oh What a Lovely War*
Timberlake Wertenbaker *Our Country's Good* • Arnold Wesker
The Merchant • Oscar Wilde *The Importance of Being Earnest*
Tennessee Williams *A Streetcar Named Desire* • *The Glass Menagerie*

Methuen Drama Modern Plays

include work by

Edward Albee
Jean Anouilh
John Arden
Margaretta D'Arcy
Peter Barnes
Sebastian Barry
Brendan Behan
Dermot Bolger
Edward Bond
Bertolt Brecht
Howard Brenton
Anthony Burgess
Simon Burke
Jim Cartwright
Caryl Churchill
Noël Coward
Lucinda Coxon
Sarah Daniels
Nick Darke
Nick Dear
Shelagh Delaney
David Edgar
David Eldridge
Dario Fo
Michael Frayn
John Godber
Paul Godfrey
David Greig
John Guare
Peter Handke
David Harrower
Jonathan Harvey
Iain Heggie
Declan Hughes
Terry Johnson
Sarah Kane
Charlotte Keatley
Barrie Keeffe
Howard Korder

Robert Lepage
Doug Lucie
Martin McDonagh
John McGrath
Terrence McNally
David Mamet
Patrick Marber
Arthur Miller
Mtwa, Ngema & Simon
Tom Murphy
Phyllis Nagy
Peter Nichols
Sean O'Brien
Joseph O'Connor
Joe Orton
Louise Page
Joe Penhall
Luigi Pirandello
Stephen Poliakoff
Franca Rame
Mark Ravenhill
Philip Ridley
Reginald Rose
Willy Russell
Jean-Paul Sartre
Sam Shepard
Wole Soyinka
Simon Stephens
Shelagh Stephenson
Peter Straughan
C. P. Taylor
Theatre de Complicite
Theatre Workshop
Sue Townsend
Judy Upton
Timberlake Wertenbaker
Roy Williams
Snoo Wilson
Victoria Wood

Methuen Drama Contemporary Dramatists

include

John Arden (two volumes)
Arden & D'Arcy
Peter Barnes (three volumes)
Sebastian Barry
Dermot Bolger
Edward Bond (eight volumes)
Howard Brenton
  (two volumes)
Richard Cameron
Jim Cartwright
Caryl Churchill
  (two volumes)
Sarah Daniels (two volumes)
Nick Darke
David Edgar (three volumes)
David Eldridge
Ben Elton
Dario Fo (two volumes)
Michael Frayn (three volumes)
John Godber (three volumes)
Paul Godfrey
David Greig
John Guare
Lee Hall (two volumes)
Peter Handke
Jonathan Harvey
  (two volumes)
Declan Hughes
Terry Johnson (three volumes)
Sarah Kane
Barrie Keeffe
Bernard-Marie Koltès
  (two volumes)
David Lan
Bryony Lavery
Deborah Levy
Doug Lucie

David Mamet (four volumes)
Martin McDonagh
Duncan McLean
Anthony Minghella
  (two volumes)
Tom Murphy (five volumes)
Phyllis Nagy
Anthony Neilson
Philip Osment
Gary Owen
Louise Page
Stewart Parker (two volumes)
Joe Penhall
Stephen Poliakoff
  (three volumes)
David Rabe
Mark Ravenhill
Christina Reid
Philip Ridley
Willy Russell
Eric-Emmanuel Schmitt
Ntozake Shange
Sam Shepard (two volumes)
Wole Soyinka (two volumes)
Simon Stephens
Shelagh Stephenson
David Storey (three volumes)
Sue Townsend
Judy Upton
Michel Vinaver
  (two volumes)
Arnold Wesker (two volumes)
Michael Wilcox
Roy Williams (two volumes)
Snoo Wilson (two volumes)
David Wood (two volumes)
Victoria Wood